THE ARCHITECTURE OF
CHICAGO'S LOOP

A GUIDE TO THE CENTRAL AND NEARBY DISTRICTS

by Frances H. Steiner

The Architecture of Chicago's Loop, A Guide to the Central and Nearby Districts
Steiner, Frances H.

Graphic design: Kristy D. Lewis, Steel Wool Design
Cover photograph: Chicago's Skyline, by Frances H. Steiner

ISBN: 0-9667259-0-5
Library of Congress catalog card number: 98-061373

Published by the Sigma Press
Batavia, Illinois, USA

Acknowledgements and Credits
Appreciation is extended for permission to publish the following photographs: To John Buck, p. 47; To the City of Chicago, Commision on Chicago Landmarks for pp. 19, 20, 21, 26, 31, and 47; To Dirk Lohan, p. 130; To Murphy-Jahn for pp. 29, 32, 37-38, 45, and 146; To Tim Olson for p. 10; To Stephen Steiner for pp. 4, 91, and 104. All other photographs are by the author. In addition, I wish to thank Chistine Happ Olson and Jon Riley for their assistance in preparing photographs and to Kristy Lewis for her design, inspiration and advise relating to the book.

Frances Steiner, September- 10, 1998

To Carl Condit, my beloved teacher, and to my students
at Dominican University, who have inspired this book by their interest, their questions,
and their enthusiasm for our field trips to the Loop.

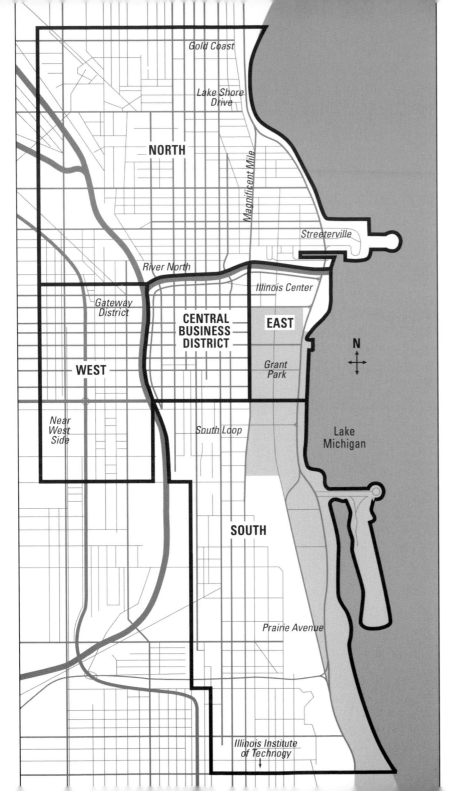

Introduction

CENTRAL BUSINESS DISTRICT

TABLE OF CONTENTS

Wellspring of urban growth and geographical center of the business district of the city, Chicago's Loop has been a proving ground for some of America's greatest architecture. The city's reputation far exceeds the shores of our continent, and for more than one hundred years, Chicago has been a Mecca for architects. It has achieved a stature architecturally comparable to that of Paris in the world of Impressionism or Cubism. The city itself is an outdoor museum, concentrated in the heart of its commercial and financial life, a magnificent array of architectural, structural and engineering marvels.

The term, "the Loop," originally referred to the route around the central business district taken by the horse cars of the 1860s and the streetcars which circled this district during the next two decades. The elevated tracks, built during the 1890s along the same route, remain today and are the subject of some controversy. Preservationists have fought for their retention, but the business community would benefit by their demise, for the massive elevated structure makes it more difficult to see the buildings. Over the years, however, as the central concentration of business has expanded in all directions, so has the definition of the Loop. To the east, high rise office and apartment buildings have been built on the air rights of the Illinois Central Railway. A flourishing of shopping, restaurant and hotel facilities has burgeoned north of the Chicago River in River North, North Michigan, and Streeterville. To the west, high office and residential buildings have been erected, and to the south, historic structures of former printing establishments have been converted to lofts, and many blocks of new housing have been built, bringing vitality back into the southern part of the Loop.

Chicago's architectural significance has much to do with its development, and to understand the greatness of our architectural heritage, it would be beneficial to consider how the city's history influenced its building. Why here? What forces were at work here which led to the construction of buildings which would attract the attention of architects throughout the world?

To begin with, geography played a role in the city's development. The site of the present Loop at the mouth of the Chicago River presented a strong advantage for future growth. The significance of the river was recognized by Father Marquette and Louis Jolliet in 1674, long before the first settlers arrived in Chicago. Jolliet suggested that a canal should be built to connect the Chicago River to the Illinois, while Marquette envisioned that a great city would be built here. Thus, from the beginning it was seen that Chicago would play a large role on the trade route between the Great Lakes and the Mississippi. The ideal siting led to phenomenal growth. Once the land had been surveyed and began to be auctioned off, the city expanded at an unprecedented rate as floods of new settlers came from the east seeking to accumulate their fortunes in the burgeoning real estate market, and immigrants arrived willing to work at hard labor in the stockyards or on the Illinois Canal. Chicago became the mid-continental hub of the railways, connecting lines which linked the Atlantic and Pacific. Situated within convenient distance of thousands of acres of farmland, it provided seeds, barbed wire, and farm implements of all kinds, including McCormick's reaper, manufactured just north of the Chicago River and east of Michigan. In addition, the stock-yards brought tremendous wealth to the city, especially late in the nineteenth century, after the development of the refrigeration car, permitting fresh meat to be shipped to all parts of the country.

The very fact that Chicago was on the frontier had much to do with its unique-ness. The settlers who were drawn here were risk-takers, ready for adven-ture and experiment, gambling on their ability to make a fortune. The frontier carpenter-builders and masons were different individuals from those of the East coast. Rarely did the early builders have much training; indeed, their cre-dentials were merely that they had apprenticed with a carpenter-builder and that they learned to follow the so-called pattern-books. Perhaps because they had little training, when their ingenuity was put to the test, they were willing to solve structural problems in an unconventional manner and with a "fresh eye." The unique contribution of the personalities of the frontier town along with the pressures of the swelling population led to unique solutions.

Chicago's first great contribution to architecture, the balloon frame, relates directly to the intense pressure of population influx. It is generally thought that Augustine D. Taylor, the carpenter who built the first St. Mary's Church in 1833, was its inventor, although there must have been numerous other balloon frame structures begun about the same time. This method of construction uti-lized light boards of 2-inch by 4-inch section, tripled at the corners and other-wise spaced 16 inches apart. The lightweight timbers replaced the heavy posts and beams typical of wood construction of the time, with the advantage

DELAWARE BUILDING

of being able to be nailed rather than having connections of hand-carved mortise-and-tenon joints. Thus, great time and material was saved. Timber frame construction today is derived from this early balloon construction.

As growth increased, each decade presented its own build-ing crises, but the ultimate crisis was the Great Chicago Fire of 1871, in which four square miles of the downtown area was gut-ted. Almost immediately, the work of reconstruction began. A frenzy of building activity began, bringing carpenters, bricklayers, stone masons and ironworkers from various parts of the city. The huge number of structures built in the next two years is notable, as well as the speed of their construction, but the styles were repetitious of the buildings of the previous decade. Nevertheless, the period brought many new faces to the architectural world and provided a maturation time, setting the stage for the drama of the late century.

A giant step forward came in the 1880s, when the city became the locale for the development of the earliest skyscrapers. Perhaps it was the "get-rich-quick" environment in Chicago, set by the earlier speculators who gravitated to the frontier, which pressured the architects to build higher and higher. Whatever the cause, new structural heights were reached here. Although William LeBaron Jenney's nine-story Home Insurance Building of 1885, no longer standing, was considered to be the first skyscraper, many other architects were involved in the evolution of multi-story construction. The chief players in this episode of Chicago's history, in addition to Jenney, were the firms of Burnham & Root, Adler & Sullivan, and Holabird & Roche. Chicago, with its liberal building codes and zoning laws, allowed the testing of new ideas; the gradual conversion from load-bearing walls to skeleton construction; the introduction of new materials such as steel and concrete; the improvement of foundations; elevators; and more effective wind-bracing and fireproofing.

With the approach of the twentieth century, architecture moved toward greater clarity of form, especially toward rectilinearity, as we can see in the work of Holabird & Roche (see the Gage Group on Michigan Avenue and the McClurg Building on Wabash). Frank Lloyd Wright's remodeling of the Rookery lobby (LaSalle Street) is a beautiful example of rectangular forms supplanting the curvilinear ones of Root's earlier design. While Wright's Prairie School became the modern expression of the mid-western suburbs, it also had an impact in some of the Loop's structures, such as in the Chapin & Gore Building, designed by Hugh Garden, working for Richard E. Schmidt. (Wabash tour).

During the 1920s, a new style of skyscraper took form, influenced by the new zoning laws. The Chicago City Council had changed building height limits numerous times between 1892 and 1920, but in 1923, they eliminated the height limit while at the same time imposing a volume limit. The purpose of the code was to ensure that sunlight would reach the street level. The result was to encourage blocky buildings which were stepped-back in wedding cake fashion. Many of these can be seen on the Magnificent Mile tour. Typical of the same period was the Art Deco, a geometric, French-influenced decorative style which shed all historical references. Chicago has some beautiful examples, such as the Palmolive Building, 333 North Michigan, and the Board of Trade.

LAKE SHORE SKYLINE

No architect has made greater impact on Chicago's skyline than Ludwig Mies van der Rohe, who came from Germany in 1939 to build a new campus at Illinois Institute of Technology and to become head of the school's architecture department. His rational philosophy—"less is more", straightforward form, and perfection of details—permeates his works and those of his students for decades to follow. The apartment buildings at 860-880 Lake Shore Drive were shocking in their simplicity and forthright display of structure when they were built. Mies' buildings in the central Loop were designed and built near the end of his career: the Federal Center, the IBM Building, and One and Two Illinois Center.

Mies' dominant presence in the city, however, is especially felt through the work of his students, graduates at IIT. Especially notable are the Richard J. Daley Center designed by Jacques Brownson for C.F. Murphy, McCormick East designed by Gene Sommers of C.F. Murphy, and Lake Point Tower by Schipporeit-Heinrich, former students and employees of Mies. Mies' followers have also been the leaders in developing new structural systems, which in turn have also impacted the city visually. Three of the partners of Skidmore, Owings & Merrill, namely Bruce Graham, Myron Goldsmith, and the structural engineer Fazlur Khan, have developed and experimented with tube construction, in which the walls of the tube, rather than a skeleton, bear the weight of the structure. The added strength allows the engineer to reduce the amount of material, thereby lowering the cost of the building. The 860 Dewitt Apartments and the Brunswick Building are reinforced concrete tubes; the Hancock Building is a steel tube, braced on the exterior; the Sears Tower is constructed as a bundle of nine tubes.

As early as the 1960s, Chicago architecture began to take another turn, partly in reaction to the simplicity of Mies. Bertrand Goldberg, who had been trained in the International Style tradition, built Marina City, with two reinforced concrete towers, scalloped with projecting balconies. These radically different forms immediately became an icon of the city. Since that time, architects have developed a myriad of unique profiles to satisfy their clients' concern for greater visibility. C.F. Murphy and Perkins & Will collaborated on a radical sweeping shape for the First National Bank Building; Perkins & Will gave the U.S. Gypsum Building a form inspired by a gypsum crystal; Harry Weese, trained in the International Style, experimented with triangular forms in a number of his Chicago buildings; and Kenzo Tange, more recently, hollowed out a space through his polygonal tower for the AMA. Post-Modernism in Chicago in the 1980s is represented especially by Helmut Jahn, who rose in the C.F. Murphy firm to become a name partner. Jahn's designs, often inspired by the Art Deco, have high visibility with unusual and even radical shapes, smooth glassy surfaces, and often intense color. The newer structures of the 1980s and 1990s exhibit much visual diversity, partly because architects from other locations have been commissioned: Kohn Pederson Fox and Johnson & Burgee of New York, Kenzo Tange and Kurokawa of Japan, Ricardo Bofill of Spain.

As one wanders the streets of the Loop today, one is ever aware of the city as a collage, with its butting together of old and new, its architectural layering of styles of the last century and a half, inevitable through the passage of time, and the juxtaposition of concepts brought here by architects from elsewhere. Although Chicago's urban fabric is more diverse now, the architectural impact of this "City of Big Shoulders" (Carl Sandburg) continues to present a bold, powerful and impressive image.

N

RANDOLPH

C23

C22

WASHINGTON

C21
C20
C19

MADISON

C18
C17 C16
C15

Grant Park

MONROE

C14
C13 C12
C11

C7

ADAMS

C10
C9
C8

JACKSON

C6
C5
C4

VAN BUREN

C3
C2
C1

CONGRESS

PLYMOUTH COURT
STATE
WABASH
MICHIGAN

C1
AUDITORIUM BUILDING
430 South Michigan

C2
FINE ARTS BUILDING
410 South Michigan

C3
CHICAGO CLUB
81 East Van Buren

C4
McCORMICK BUILDING
332 South Michigan

C5
318 SOUTH MICHIGAN

C6
BRITANNICA CENTER
320 South Michigan

C7
ART INSTITUTE OF CHICAGO
201 South Michigan

C8
SANTA FE CENTER
430 South Michigan

C9
SYMPHONY CENTER
220 South Michigan

C10
BORG-WARNER BUILDING
200 South Michigan

C11
PEOPLE'S GAS COMPANY
BUILDING
122 South Michigan

C12
LAKE VIEW BUILDING
116 South Michigan

C13
112 SOUTH MICHIGAN

C14
MONROE BUILDING
104 South Michigan

C15
UNIVERSITY CLUB
76 East Monroe

C16
GAGE GROUP
18 South Michigan

C17
CHICAGO ATHLETIC
ASSOCIATION
12 South Michigan

C18
WILLOUGHBY TOWER
8 South Michigan

C19
TOWER BUILDING
6 North Michigan

C20
BURRELL BUILDING
20 North Michigan

C21
MICHIGAN AVENUE BUILDING
30 North Michigan

C22
CULTURAL CENTER
78 East Washington

C23
STONE CONTAINER BUILDING
150 North Michigan

MICHIGAN AVENUE

Michigan Avenue is a good place to begin a tour of the Loop, for its buildings are lined up soldier-like, facing the park and the lake, and perhaps welcoming the visitor to the city. In the nineteenth century, the waterfront was much closer, and Michigan Avenue would have been the first glimpse of the city for passengers arriving by ship. Most of the Michigan Avenue skyline, as seen from Grant Park today, is turn-of-the-century, dating from 1885 to World War I. The continuity of the structures was primarily due to the efforts of Daniel Burnham in the 1890s and early 20th century. He helped select the architects in 1892 for the Cultural Center and the Art Institute; he designed a large number of buildings on the street; he did much to set the taste for a neo-classical revival; and he set forth in his Chicago Plan of 1909 ideals of regularity, uniformity, and large cultural foci. Finally, Burnham moved his office to the Railway Exchange (Santa Fe Center) on Michigan Avenue, from which he watched and supervised the construction of Grant Park.

AUDITORIUM BUILDING

C1
AUDITORIUM BUILDING
430 South Michigan
Adler & Sullivan, 1887-89

With this great building—the opera house of Chicago until 1829—Louis Sullivan's reputation was established, both in the United States and in Europe. Sullivan's aesthetic genius combined with Dankbar Adler's expertise and instinct in regard to acoustics and engineering to make this one of the greatest buildings of its era. An immense building for its time, it combined several functions with the Auditorium Hotel (now Roosevelt University) on Michigan Avenue, the theater on Congress, and offices on the Wabash Avenue section as well as in the tower.

Dankbar Adler, who had considerable experience in designing theaters, was responsible for the building's acoustics, which have received much acclaim. Adler solved many other difficult engineering problems here as well, such as the design of massive raft foundations with steel rails in concrete to accommodate the greater weight of the tower. He devised a system of lifting the stage in sections hydraulically and of cooling the auditorium by pumping cold air through vents.

Sullivan was responsible for the design of the facades and the elaborate interiors. The first three of the building's ten stories are built of rusticated granite, while the upper facades are of ashlar limestone. Tremendous wide arches with long voussoirs and low proportions serve as triple entrances on Michigan and Congress. The facades have complex rhythms, which reflect an earlier building that he admired: the Marshall Field Wholesale Store by H.H. Richardson.

The Roosevelt University lobby on Michigan Avenue provides some idea of the splendor of Sullivan's design. A dado of Mexican onyx six feet high lines the walls. Large columns are clad in scagliola, painted plasterwork imitating marble. Ornament abounds in stenciled fabric on the ceiling, in plaster work of the arches, in the mosaics of the floor, and in the newel posts and iron railings of the grand staircase. Two important restored Sullivan interiors in this building are the small Rudolf Ganz Recital Hall on the seventh floor and the library, formerly the hotel dining room, on the tenth floor.

Sullivan's crowning achievement was the theater itself. The great space is spanned by a series of elliptical arches, each lined with a series of tiny jewel-like electric bulbs. Gilded ornamentation is focused especially around the stage. Abundant foliage and geometric patterns are intertwined and surround panels holding names of various composers. The young Frank Lloyd Wright, working in the firm since 1887, drew much of the auditorium's ornament under Sullivan's supervision. The foliated patterns take on a liveliness exceeding Sullivan's earlier work, although not so flowing as his later ornament, such as that in the Carson, Pirie, Scott Building. This is truly one of the most spectacular interiors in America.

FINE ARTS BUILDING

C2
FINE ARTS BUILDING
410 South Michigan
Solon S. Beman, 1885 and 1898

S. S. Beman was commissioned in 1884 by the Studebaker Brothers to design a showroom for their carriages and wagons, which were manufactured in South Bend, Indiana. His solution was a somewhat exotic Romanesque facade of five bays with red Hollowell granite walls at the base and rusticated Bedford limestone on the upper floors. The four lower stories were provided with large windows to serve as showrooms. Large granite pillars flank the entrance and separate the bays of the third and fourth floors. The original roof stood in a pyramidal form with conical caps.

In 1898, the Studebaker Brothers decided to have Beman design another showroom on South Wabash. Beman also received the commission to remodel their original building to include artists' studios, shops, offices and theaters. The facade of the upper floor was removed and replaced with a three-story addition, a flat roof, and a terra cotta and copper cornice. Since this remodeling, the building has served the needs of artists and musicians.

C3
CHICAGO CLUB
81 East Van Buren
Granger & Bollenbachker, 1930

Before the Art Institute moved into its building across the street, it occupied a four-story Romanesque building on this site designed by Burnham & Root. The Chicago Club, a private men's organization, purchased the building in 1892 and occupied it until 1929, when it collapsed in remodeling. The present structure was built in the Italian Romanesque style, incorporating the entrance of the Burnham & Root building into their Van Buren Street facade.

C4
McCORMICK BUILDING
332 South Michigan
Holabird & Roche, 1910-1912

Less progressive than most of Holabird & Roche's architecture of this period, this 20-story steel frame structure was built for Robert Hall McCormick, the nephew of Cyrus McCormick, the manufacturer of farm machinery. Constructed in two stages to the highest limit permitted by code, its aesthetic is a Renaissance palazzo type with plain Roman brick walls and a heavy bracketed Italian cornice.

C5
318 SOUTH MICHIGAN
Anonymous Architect, 1885 and 1911; Nagle, Hartray & Associates, 1982

This beautiful facade in the Italian Renaissance revival style was created in three stages. Little remains except the basic structure from the original 1885 building. All the terra cotta work of the upper stories is from the 1911 renovation, including the four-story Ionic pilasters and the seventh-story arcade. Nagle, Hartray & Associates refaced the lower two stories in rusticated limestone.

318 SOUTH MICHIGAN

C6
BRITANNICA CENTER
320 South Michigan
Graham, Anderson, Probst & White, 1923-24

Originally built for the banking firm S. W. Straus & Co., this eclectic 30-story structure took advantage of a zoning law passed in Chicago in 1923, which allowed much greater heights if set-backs were used. The major part of the building is a 21-story block, which is then surmounted by a slender tower of seven stories, and finally reduces in size for the top two stories. The structure, topped with a stepped pyramid surmounted by a blue glass beehive, has become a trademark of the Chicago skyline.

Room, the work of Adler & Sullivan, salvaged from the demolished Stock Exchange Building and installed in the Art Institute by John Vinci in 1977. The latest major addition is the Rice Building by Hammond, Beeby & Babka, a restrained, but free interpretation of the classical style.

C8
SANTA FE CENTER
224 South Michigan
D.H. Burnham & Co.,1904; Renovation by Metz, Train, & Youngren, 1984

Sheathed in glistening cream terra cotta with delicate Renaissance detailing, this 17-story office structure is square in plan with a rectangular light court. On its facade, pilasters face the piers, alternating with show windows on the street level, and with bay windows from the fourth to the thirteenth stories. The top story forms a frieze of circular openings providing a visual termination for the facades. Burnham, whose offices were on the top floor, enjoyed watching the execution in Grant Park of parts of his 1909 Plan of Chicago. Be sure to visit the beautifully restored lobby, where the Chicago Architecture Foundation is now located.

C7
ART INSTITUTE OF CHICAGO
201 South Michigan
Shepley, Rutan & Coolidge, 1890-92; Morton Wing: Shaw, Metz & Associates, 1962; Rice Building: Hammond, Beeby & Babka, 1988

The Art Institute's opening coincided with that of the World's Columbian Exposition. The museum's grand Italian Renaissance facade has a tripartite arrangement with a pedimented 5-bayed central section projecting forward and seven-bayed wings on either side. Above the arcaded entry loggia in the rusticated base of the structure are three grand Palladian arches separated by Corinthian half-columns. Bronze lions by Chicago sculptor Edward Kemys, shown on Coolidge's original drawings, flank the museum. Extending to the north and south are the later Ferguson and Morton Wings. Of special interest also is the classical McKinlock Court, in the center of which is a beautiful fountain with bronze sea creatures by Swedish sculptor Carl Milles. Another area not to miss is the reconstructed Stock Exchange Trading

SYMPHONY CENTER

C9
SYMPHONY CENTER
220 South Michigan
D.H. Burnham & Co., 1904, 1908; Renovation, Skidmore, Owings & Merrill, 1996

Daniel Burnham, who served as vice-president of the Orchestral Association, raised thousands of dollars toward the building of this concert hall and waived his design fee. The facade is an elegant Renaissance revival design of red brick in Flemish bond with Georgian sash windows and limestone quoins. Three immense arched windows dominate the *piano nobile* reception level. Above the Italianate cornice, recessed behind a balustrade, was once the Cliffdwellers Club, where Louis Sullivan spent much time in his later years. In the recent renovation, at a cost of $105 million, the roof was raised 36 feet above the proscenium arch, an acoustical crown constructed, and additional space for a variety of functions to the north and west added.

C10
BORG-WARNER BUILDING
200 South Michigan
A. Epstein & Sons; William E. Lescaze, Associate Architect, 1958

This 22-story, steel-cage office structure has a bright blue aluminum curtain wall which seems out of place among the early twentieth century buildings which surround it. It replaced the Pullman Building, a heavy rusticated granite Romanesque structure by S.S. Beman.

C11
PEOPLE'S GAS COMPANY BUILDING
122 South Michigan
D.H. Burnham & Co.,1907-1911

Built to the maximum height permitted at the time (260 feet), this 20-story office building is ornate and eclectic, having Greek, Roman, Egyptian, Renaissance and Baroque details. A large-scale colonnade of full-rounded, monolithic polished granite columns lines the street facades, mirrored at the 18th story by a terra cotta colonnade. Notice the garland-framed oval windows over entrances and the antefixes on the roof.

C12
LAKE VIEW BUILDING
116 South Michigan
Jenney, Mundie & Jensen, 1906 and 1912

Originally known as the Municipal Court Building, the structure was built as twelve stories, to which four more were added six years later by the same architects. Its slender, 3-bay facade is sheathed in white glazed terra cotta, ornamented with restrained classical details. Paired sash windows fill the bays.

C13
112 SOUTH MICHIGAN
(Formerly the Illinois Athletic Club)
Barnett, Haynes & Barnett of St. Louis, 1907; Addition and renovation: Swann & Weiskopf, 1985

The Illinois Athletic Club was originally a twelve-story structure in the Italianate Renaissance style sheathed in Bedford limestone above a gray granite base. The blocks of stone are up to eight feet high. Just below the original cornice is a wide frieze of chariots and life-sized figures in various forms of athletic activity, executed in a classical manner by Henne & Co. of Chicago. In 1985 the interior was remodeled and six stories were added above the original cornice.

C14
MONROE BUILDING
104 South Michigan
Holabird & Roche, 1912

Between the University Club and the Charlie Club, the 16-story Monroe Building was designed to harmonize with its neighbors. Like the University Club, it has a gable roof with a two-story attic. The Monroe is Italian Gothic in style rather than English, sheathed in terra cotta above its polished red granite base. Its facades are ornamented with quatrafoils in the spandrels and massive moldings on the piers. Large arched windows and spiral colonnettes fill the gable walls from the thirteenth story to the roof. Don't miss the lobby with its walls and Gothic vaulted ceiling which are covered with Rockwood pottery tiles in patterns blending with those of the exterior.

C15
UNIVERSITY CLUB
76 East Monroe
Holabird & Roche, 1909

Built as a private men's club, this 14-story tower is in the English collegiate Gothic style, complete with elaborate tracery, balconies and intricate pinnacles. The limestone facades are carved under the direction of a Chicago sculptor, John Tait, with vines, masks, symbols of learning in shields, and gargoyles which extend nine feet from the surface of the wall. The interior is notable for its Michigan Room on the second floor, with painted panels by Frederick Clay Bartlett; the eighth floor library; and the ninth floor vaulted Cathedral Hall.

UNIVERSITY CLUB

C16
GAGE GROUP

18 South Michigan
Holabird & Roche with Louis Sullivan, 1898

While often called the Gage Group, the three buildings at 18, 24 and 30 South Michigan were actually built for Stanley McCormick and leased to three millinery manufacturers: Gage, Keith and Ascher. Louis Sullivan, following his breakup with Adler, designed the terra cotta facade of the northernmost building, leased by Gage, which originally had an elaborate cast iron base of exuberant flowing foliage ornament. The two central piers rise like giant stems to the summit where they appear to burst forth in clusters of sprawling foliage. Originally eight stories, it was increased to twelve in 1902.

CHICAGO ATHLETIC ASSOCIATION

C17
CHICAGO ATHLETIC ASSOCIATION

12 South Michigan
Henry Ives Cobb, 1891-3; Addition at 71 E. Madison Street by Richard E. Schmidt, 1906

This ten-story, private club is a beautiful example of the Venetian Gothic revival style. The red brick and cream-colored limestone facade is extremely varied with interlacing and overlapping arches, two-story columns, diaper patterns and quatrefoil tracery. In 1906 a twelve-story addition was designed by Hugh Garden, who worked in the firm of Richard Schmidt. In 1926, six more stories were added to the addition by Schmidt, Garden & Martin.

GAGE GROUP

C18
WILLOUGHBY TOWER

8 South Michigan
Samuel N. Crowen, 1929

This 36-story Gothic revival tower has a blocky base with a very slender turreted tower. Sheathing is Indiana limestone surmounted on a base of gray granite. Its original, finely-appointed lobby remains intact.

C19
TOWER BUILDING

6 North Michigan
Richard D. Schmidt, 1898

Built for Montgomery Ward as headquarters for his mail order company, this 390-foot structure was for a time the tallest in Chicago. It has lost its original pyramidal roof as well as the gilded nude female statue, *Progress Lighting the Way for Commerce,* which stood atop it. Hugh Garden, a young architect in Schmidt's firm, collaborated on the design, although the carved marble classical ornament which originally adorned the 3-story base is surprisingly different from Garden's later work. From this building Montgomery Ward oversaw the activities of Grant Park and sought to protect public land from encroachment.

C20
BURRELL BUILDING

20 North Michigan
Beers, Clay & Dutton, 1885; Addition, 1892; Renovation by Nagle, Hartray & Associates, 1985

This converted warehouse, which originally belonged to Montgomery Ward, was a five-story, three-bay structure. Soon it doubled in size, and in 1892, three additional stories were added. The clarity and openness of its facade is a foretaste of the Chicago functionalism of the turn-of-the-century. Nagle, Hartray & Associates have tastefully renovated the structure for office use, giving it a large cut-out entry and an eight-story atrium with a skylight. On the exterior they dressed the structure with a limestone-faced base and large shell-like accents above the cornice.

C21
MICHIGAN AVENUE BUILDING

30 North Michigan Avenue
Jarvis Hunt, 1914

This 15-story Gothic revival structure was originally planned to have a 14-story tower, but since a 200-foot height restriction existed in 1914, the tower was put on hold. Five stories were added in 1923. The exterior terra cotta facades are enlivened with an alternating rhythm of narrow rounded mullions and wider piers.

BURRELL BUILDING

CULTURAL CENTER

STONE CONTAINER BUILDING

C22
CULTURAL CENTER
78 East Washington
Shepley, Rutan & Coolidge, 1897

The Chicago Cultural Center was built on a square block which had been Chicago's first public land, Dearborn Park. The four-story building appears to be two-story. Its granite base is surmounted by walls of blue Bedford limestone. Originally the north part of the building, with its Greek Revival portico, housed the GAR, an organization of Union soldiers and sailors; while the south portion of the building, serving as public library, was entered through a Renaissance Revival portico. Shepley, Rutan & Coolidge, inheritors of H.H. Richardson's Boston firm, specialized in the Renaissance revival style. Their design for the library relates to that of the Art Institute, which was begun about the same time.

The south lobby of the structure is a palatial space with a grand stairway of white Carrara marble leading to a magnificent room on the third floor, crowned by a Tiffany favrile glass dome, one of Chicago's most splendid interiors. Holabird and Root, in a skillful renovation in 1977, modified the structure to serve as a center for speakers, exhibits, recitals and various cultural events.

C23
STONE CONTAINER BUILDING
150 North Michigan
A. Epstein & Sons, 1983

Wrapped in bands of white aluminum and reflective glass, this striking building has a roofline which slopes dramatically over a ten-story height on a 54-degree angle toward Grant Park, accommodating itself visually to the turn of the corner at the northwest end of the park. Just back of the slope are five two-story atriums. To prevent an avalanche due to snow accumulation, designer Sheldon Schlegman devised a system of feeding 120-degree water onto the slope to melt the snow, when necessary. On street level, Yaacov Agam's sculpture *Communication X9* provides an island of color and contrast.

N

LAKE

C24

RANDOLPH

WASHINGTON
C25

C26

MADISON
C27 C28

C29
C31
C30
C33 C32

MONROE

C34

ADAMS

C35
C36

C37

JACKSON

C38

VAN BUREN

C39

CONGRESS

PLYMOUTH COURT
STATE
WABASH
MICHIGAN

Grant Park

C24
SELF-PARK
60 East Lake

C25
MARSHALL FIELD & CO.
*Northwest corner, Washington
and Wabash*

C26
PITTSFIELD BUILDING
55 East Washington

C27
14 NORTH WABASH

C28
5 NORTH WABASH

C29
HEYWORTH BUILDING
8 South Wabash

C30
SILVERSMITH BUILDING
10 South Wabash

C31
JEWELERS BUILDING
15-19 South Wabash

C32
CHAMPLAIN BUILDING
37 South Wabash

C33
CARSON PIRIE SCOTT & CO.
ADDITIONS
18-24 South Wabash

C34
MID-CONTINENTAL PLAZA
55 East Monroe

C35
CHAPIN & GORE BUILDING
63 East Adams

C36
McCLURG BUILDING
218 South Wabash

C37
STEGER BUILDING
28 East Jackson

C38
CNA CENTER
55 East Jackson

C39
RICHARDSON BUILDING
*Northwest corner of Wabash
and Congress*

WABASH AVENUE

From Lake Street to Congress

by The character of Wabash Avenue was established by at least the 1880s as a street of small retail and wholesale shops, especially dealing in jewelry or musical instruments. Even today it retains numerous jewelers' shops, especially those in the so-called "Jewelers' Row," the block between Monroe and Madison. *The Economist* reported in 1895 that there were at least twenty large houses engaged in manufacturing or selling musical instruments in a two or three block stretch on Wabash, including W.W. Kimball and Lyon & Healy. The street was never able to achieve the prominence of State Street or Michigan Avenue, however, partly because of the presence of the Elevated tracks, which were built in 1893.

SELF-PARK

C24
SELF-PARK
60 East Lake
Tigerman Fugman McCurry, 1986

Stanley Tigerman, who delights in bringing humor into architecture, once said, "There is more to Life than Less," contradicting Mies's "Less is More." The ten-story Self-Park, which can be thought of as "Pop Architecture", resembles a classic Rolls Royce. One can't help but be amused at the facade which takes the form of an automobile grille, the awnings over the doorways which refer to fenders, the painted surfaces imitating the patterns of tire treads, and even the "hood ornament" at the top. Without question, the building speaks of the relationship between its architectural form and the parking function.

C25
MARSHALL FIELD & CO.
Northwest corner, Washington and Wabash
D.H. Burnham & Co., 1892

The earliest section of the department store as it stands today was designed by Charles Atwood working in the firm of D.H. Burnham. It is a nine-story block which has more ornate facades than the rest of the store. At the time of its erection, *Engineering News* described it as "probably the costliest building of the size and kind in the city."

C26
PITTSFIELD BUILDING
55 East Washington
Graham, Anderson, Probst & White, 1927

In 1927 the 38-story Pittsfield Building claimed to be Chicago's tallest skyscraper. Its windows rise in vertical bands between limestone-clad mullions springing from a polished black granite base. Its details are Gothic, but the overall effect is Art Deco. The main entrance on Washington leads through an elevator lobby to a five-story court onto which face interior shop windows.

C27
14 NORTH WABASH
(Formerly Mandel Brothers Annex)
Holabird & Roche, 1900, 1905

This turn-of-the-century department store, later occupied by the Wieboldt Store, represents a bold expression of the steel skeleton. Unlike most Chicago School buildings, the emphasis here is on the horizontal rather than the vertical. Its spandrels have geometric moldings which project beyond the piers and carry the eye from one bay to the next. The top three stories were added in 1905.

C28
5 NORTH WABASH
(Formerly the Kesner Building)
Jenney, Munsen & Jensen, 1910

A terra cotta base is surmounted by a pressed brick shaft. The top, or 17th story, forms an ornamental terra cotta frieze surmounted by an elaborate cornice. *Construction News* reported that this was "the most speedily constructed building ever erected in Chicago." The steel cage construction rests on 43 caissons.

C29
HEYWORTH BUILDING

8 South Wabash
D.H. Burnham & Co., 1905

An especially fine example of the Chicago School, the 18-story Heyworth Building clearly expresses its steel skeleton. Its facades are sheathed in beautiful terra cotta panels molded in intricate geometricized foliage designs. The patterns combine influences from the Baroque, Renaissance and Prairie school. The top three stories are visually grouped with triple arches and three-story colonnettes in each bay.

C30
SILVERSMITH BUILDING

10 South Wabash
D.H. Burnham & Co., 1897

This interesting and unusual early skyscraper attests to Burnham's creative versatility in his adaptation of architectural styles. Romanesque engaged colonnettes of molded pressed brick with foliated terra cotta capitals travel from the third story to the summit. An alternating rhythm is created by the colonnettes serving as mullions and functioning as piers. Although the structure makes strong reference to the past, it is beautiful in its clarity of organization and crispness of detail.

C31
JEWELERS BUILDING

15-19 South Wabash
Adler & Sullivan, 1882

The oldest Sullivan-designed structure in downtown Chicago, this rare example provides a glimpse of the young architect in search of a style. The use of brick with terra cotta and geometricized floral patterns demonstrate a debt to the Aesthetic Movement in England, as well as to Frank Furness of Philadelphia, for whom Sullivan once worked. The structure, built as a store and office building for Martin A. Ryerson, is largely iron. The design is complex with a wide central bay and narrower side bays, a formula typical of a number of Sullivan's early works.

SILVERSMITH BUILDING

JEWELERS BUILDING

C32
CHAMPLAIN BUILDING

(Formerly the Powers Building)
37 South Wabash
Holabird & Roche, 1903

No architectural firm at the turn-of-the-century was more successful and consistent in clearly expressing their buildings' structures than was Holabird & Roche. Continuous gray brick piers rise from the mezzanine to the cornice above the 13th story. Deeply set spandrels with unusually large Chicago windows fill each bay, creating a uniform grid facade. Brick corbel work forms delicate patterns in the piers, spandrels and especially the cornice. The building now functions as part of the School of the Art Institute.

C33
CARSON PIRIE SCOTT & CO. ADDITIONS

18-24 S. Wabash
Haskell & Barker Buildings, Wheelock & Thomas, 1875
28 S. Wabash
J.P. Atwater Building, John M. Van Osdel, 1877
Northwest corner of Monroe
Men's Store, Burnham Brothers, 1927

The Men's Store addition to the Carson's store is a modification of the formula used by Sullivan on State and Madison Streets. Just to the north of the men's store are three Italianate revival stores, also part of Carson's.

C34
MID-CONTINENTAL PLAZA

55 East Monroe
Alfred Shaw & Associates, 1972

Filling the block between Monroe and Adams Streets, this 50-story tower is out of scale with the rest of Wabash Avenue. Mostly gray inside and out, it is clad on the exterior with aluminum, and the lobby walls and floors are of granite. It has three floors of shops, 9 floors of parking and 39 floors of offices.

C35
CHAPIN & GORE BUILDING

63 East Adams
Richard E. Schmidt, 1904

Hugh Garden, who began working for Schmidt in 1901, designed this beautiful eight-story brick building before he became a partner in the firm. Because the whiskey company, which commissioned the building, required storage space on the second and third stories, the structure was built to carry 250 pounds per square foot at these levels, while the upper stories are each designed to carry 100 pounds. The facade reflects the different functions in its fenestration. Garden is especially accomplished in his ornament, which is some of the finest of the Prairie School. The Chicago Symphony Orchestra, current owner of the building, has recently gutted the interior and reconstructed the facade at street level, including the entrance to what was originally the Nepeenauk Bar, although the delicacy of Garden's ornament has been lost.

CHAPIN & GORE BUILDING

M^cCLURG BUILDING

C36
M^cCLURG BUILDING
(Also called Ayer or Crown Building)
218 South Wabash
Holabird & Roche, 1899

The McClurg Building is a clear expression of its steel skeleton. The walls of the 3-bay structure are largely glass. Its restrained ornament in cream terra cotta emphasizes the verticality of the piers, which project beyond the spandrels. Egyptoid half-colonnettes mask the two center piers while quarter-colonnettes are on the side piers. This 9-story structure is one of the best examples of the work of Holabird & Roche, and of the Chicago School of architecture.

C37
STEGER BUILDING
28 East Jackson
Marshall & Fox, 1909

Built for a piano manufacturer, this French Renaissance style building has a base of dark green polished granite surmounted by enameled terra cotta. Brick covers the walls from the 4th to the 17th stories, above which the top story is ornamented with terra cotta. *Construction News* in 1910 claimed that this was the "first building in Chicago faced with enameled brick."

Compare the Steger to the DePaul University Building (formerly that of Lyon & Healy) across the street at 243 South Wabash, built by the same architects five years later.

C38
CNA CENTER
55 East Jackson, C.F. Murphy Associates, 1962
Annex, *325 S. Wabash,* Graham, Anderson, Probst & White, 1972

These two red-painted steel office buildings are both annexes to the 1924 Continental Insurance Building at 310 South Michigan. The annex at 55 East Jackson, designed by Jacques Brownson, is elegant in its crisp detailing. Heavy steel girders with welded connections form long spans between the piers. The weight of the structure and the strength of the welds of the deep girders made wind bracing unnecessary. The building was not originally planned to be red, but after using a red rust preventative, it was decided to keep the color and to paint the later annex to match.

C39
RICHARDSON BUILDING
(Originally the Kimball Building)
Northwest corner of Wabash and Congress
Anonymous Architect, 1886

Originally built as a six-story warehouse, this brick and terra cotta structure is well-proportioned and typical of its time period. Downtown Chicago was largely a brick city in the 1880s.

N

LAKE

C52

C51

RANDOLPH

C50

WASHINGTON

C49 C48

C46 C47

MADISON

C45 C44

MONROE

C43

ADAMS

JACKSON

C42

VAN BUREN

C40 C41

CONGRESS

CLARK
FEDERAL
DEARBORN
PLYMOUTH COURT
STATE
WABASH
MICHIGAN

C40
HAROLD WASHINGTON
LIBRARY
400 South State

C41
ONE CONGRESS CENTER
403 South State

C42
DEPAUL CENTER
333 South State

C43
PALMER HOUSE HOTEL
State Street and Monroe

C44
CARSON, PIRIE SCOTT
STORE
1 South State

C45
CHICAGO BUILDING
7 West Madison

C46
STATE MADISON BUILDING
22 West Madison

C47
MANDEL BROTHERS STORE
1 North State

C48
STEVENS BUILDING
17 North State

C49
RELIANCE BUILDING
32 North State

C50
MARSHALL FIELD & CO.
111 North State

C51
CHICAGO THEATER
175 North State

C52
PAGE BUILDING
175 North State

STATE STREET

State Street, nicknamed "that Great Street," is central to downtown Chicago in that the city's numbering system starts here. Its role as the major shopping thoroughfare in the city was established just after the Civil War, due almost single-handedly to the efforts of one man. Potter Palmer, the "merchant prince", bought 3/4 of a mile along State Street, built a hotel and other rentable property, and built a large department store which he rented to Field, Leiter & Co., the ancestor of Marshall Field & Co. In more recent years, the street has struggled to maintain its market share, competing with the newer shopping developments on Michigan Avenue north of the river.

C40
HAROLD WASHINGTON LIBRARY CENTER
400 South State
Hammond, Beeby & Babka, 1991

One of the most controversial of Chicago buildings, the public library design was the result of an international competition, which had so many attached stipulations that only six local architectural teams submitted designs. Each entry for the $400 million library was a design-and-build proposal in which each architect was associated with contractors and sub-contractors, so that construction would be contained within budget.

The shape of the massive structure with its tall arched windows suggests a 19th century railway station or even ancient Roman baths. It has no scale until one notices the nearby 10- or 12-story skyscrapers. The architects chose red brick and granite sheathing with red terra cotta ornament to relate the design to Chicago's historical buildings. In actuality the structure provides a counterpoint to Chicago's rational tradition, since the city's old skyscrapers were Romanesque in style rather than Roman, and the whimsical, gigantic antefixes, now causing the building to settle unevenly, give the building a Disneyland character.

C41
ONE CONGRESS CENTER
(Formerly Leiter Building II)
403 South State
William LeBaron Jenney, 1891

This building is widely published in architectural history books, not because it was the first skyscraper, or the first steel one, or the tallest one, but because in 1891, the immense structure most clearly reflected its steel skeleton. Granite pilasters sheathe the wide-spaced steel piers of the frame. The bays, filled almost entirely with glass, offer variety with sometimes eight windows per bay, sometimes four, and at the top level, six windows per bay. Romanesque colonnettes form mullions between the windows. One can read at the top of the State Street facade, "L.Z. LEITER, AD MDCCCXCI". This building, from the beginning was meant to be flexible in plan, so that it could be rented to a single store, or to as many as nine separate stores. It was first leased to a retailer, Siegel, Cooper & Co.; later it was operated as Leiter Shops; and still later it was Sears, Roebuck & Co.

C42
DEPAUL CENTER
333 South State
Holabird & Roche, 1906, 1912
Daniel P. Coffey & Associates, adaptive reuse

Built as the Rothchild Department Store, it was later the Davis Store and then Goldblatt's Department Store. The massive structure, filling the block between Jackson and Van Buren, exhibits visual clarity and conforms to the three-part organization so typical of Chicago skyscrapers. The two-story base is an arcade of display windows; the eight upper stories reflect the cellular grid of the steel skeleton; while the whole is topped by a large cornice. In the renovation, Coffey redesigned the north facade and created a variety of lively interior spaces, including shops and restaurants into its long atrium-style interior corridor, with offices and classrooms on upper levels.

C43
PALMER HOUSE HOTEL
State and Monroe
Holabird & Roche, 1923-25, 1927

The Palmer House Hotel, site of three previous nineteenth-century hotels owned by Potter Palmer, faces State Street, Madison and Wabash Avenue. A shopping arcade through the building joins the three entrances on the ground level. Two of Chicago's most distinctive interior spaces are the Empire style lobby, reached from the arcade by escalator, and the Empire Room restaurant, adjoining.

C44
CARSON, PIRIE SCOTT STORE
1 South State
Louis H. Sullivan, 1899,1904; Addition by D.H. Burnham, 1906; Addition by Holabird & Root, 1961; Restoration by John Vinci, 1979

One of Chicago's most prized landmarks is the Carson, Pirie Scott Building, originally built for Schlesinger & Mayer. The store embodies Sullivan's philosophy of "form follows function." The upper walls reflect the functional space they enclose, while the decorative panels at street level entice the pedestrian and invite shoppers to view the displays and enter. A rounded entrance projects onto the sidewalk, announcing the department store's presence.

The first section of the store was built on Madison Street in 1899, three bays wide and nine stories high. The building was extended with a 12-story unit in eight bays, one wrapping the corner and seven along State Street. The store, at what is known as the "world's busiest corner", was purchased by Carson, Pirie Scott in 1904 before this section was complete. An additional five bays were added on State Street by D.H. Burnham in 1906, and three additional bays by Holabird & Root in 1961.

The glorious cast iron ornament has a richness and almost jewel-like intricacy which is surprising in architecture. The lavish, organic vegetative forms swell and curl with flowing rhythms. The upper walls, of white terra cotta, exhibit an aesthetic which clearly reflects its grid-like skeleton frame, and anticipates the architecture of the decades to come. The "Chicago windows" are of wide proportions, and their horizontality is further emphasized by subtle bands of ornament which run continuously above and below.

CARSON, PIRIE SCOTT STORE

C45
CHICAGO BUILDING

7 West Madison
Holabird & Roche, 1904

Originally the Chicago Savings Bank Building, this 15-story office tower, sheathed in brown brick and terra cotta, boldly reflects its steel skeleton structure. The facade facing State Street has continuous vertical projecting piers with recessed spandrels and Chicago windows, while the Madison Street side has projecting bays which alternate with flat ones.

C46
STATE MADISON BUILDING
(Formerly Boston Store)

22 West Madison
Holabird & Roche, 1905-1917

This large structure, fronting on State, Madison and Dearborn, held the Boston Store, which was a retail department store until 1948, when it was converted to multi-commercial use. Its seventeen stories have large cellular bays with Chicago windows and terra cotta sheathing. The upper three floors are colonnaded. In 1974, a piece of terra cotta fell and killed a pedestrian, causing much concern in the business community about the liability caused by terra cotta cornices.

C47
MANDEL BROTHERS STORE

1 North State
Holabird & Roche, 1912

The 15-story State Street store replaced an earlier Mandel Brothers Store. Thus, this structure is more recent than its 1905 annex on Wabash. Note the granite pilasters framing the display windows at the base and the Corinthian colonnade at the top.

C48
STEVENS BUILDING

17 North State
D.H. Burnham & Co., 1912

Burnham's 19-story Stevens Building once housed the six-story Charles A. Stevens department story with offices above. The building faces Wabash as well as State Street and has an arcade connecting the two retail units.

C49
RELIANCE BUILDING

32 North State
D.H. Burnham & Company, 1895

Of all the early skyscrapers, the Reliance stands out as first to assume an aesthetic of transparency, prophetic of twentieth century architecture. It is a slender, 14-story tower, sheathed in a curtain wall of glass and white terra cotta, hanging on an all-steel skeleton. John Root, Burnham's partner until Root's untimely death in 1891, had designed a fifteen-story tower for this site in 1890. The design, now lost, was postponed because of unexpired tenant leases, after which Burnham engaged a new chief designer, Charles Atwood. E. C. Shankland, the building's engineer, introduced several innovations in skeleton construction. The steel members forming the columns were in staggered two-story lengths and in 1894, the erection of the steel skeleton took only fifteen days. Although close observation reveals bands of Gothic ornament in the terra cotta, the openness of form and vertical rhythms of the undulating walls take visual precedence. The windows are "Chicago" type, in which fixed glass alternates with movable sash.

C50
MARSHALL FIELD & CO.
111 North State
D.H. Burnham & Co., 1902, 1906, 1907, 1914

Marshall Field's retail department store business occupied the northeast corner of Washington and State since 1868, at which time he was in partnership with Levi Leiter. The grand department store today, occupying the entire block surrounded by State, Washington, Wabash and Randolph, was built in five sections, between 1892 and 1914. The 12-story State Street facade was built between 1902 and 1907. The decoration is classical, including four Ionic columns of Carrara marble flanking the State Street entrance and a two-story Corinthian colonnade on top. The magnificent light courts on the interior, which perhaps form the most impressive aspect of the architecture, were probably influenced by those of the *Bon Marche* or A*u Printemps* department stores in Paris. A six-story court at the southwest section of the store is topped by a colored mosaic dome, designed by Louis Comfort Tiffany. A more restrained 12-story court with a glass skylight is at the northeast part of the structure.

C51
CHICAGO THEATER
175 North State
Rapp & Rapp, 1921

The Chicago Theater's immense marquee and neon sign can be seen blocks away. Behind the sign is a Baroque terra cotta facade with a huge arched Tiffany stained glass window carrying the crest of Balaban and Katz, a theater company-which originally owned the building. The Grand Lobby, open to the public, gives access to the Page Building offices as well as to the theater.

C52
PAGE BUILDING
175 North State
John Van Osdel, 1871

The Lake Street facade of the Page Brothers' building is constructed of prefabricated cast iron panels. The system of construction was typical of many pre-fire buildings along Lake Street, although cast iron began to lose its favor after the fire. Housed in the building was the Page Brothers' wholesale leather company, facing Lake Street, and a wine company facing State Street. Access to the building is now through the Chicago Theater Building.

CHICAGO THEATER

N

LAKE

RANDOLPH

| C73 |
| C72 |
| C71 |

| C70 |

WASHINGTON

| C69 | C68 |
| C67 | |

MADISON

| C66 | |
| | C65 |

MONROE

| C63 | C64 |

| C61 | C62 |

ADAMS

| C60 | C60 |

JACKSON

C59	C58
		C57
		C56

| C55 |

VAN BUREN

| C54 |

| C53 |

CONGRESS

WELLS · FINANCIAL · LASALLE · CLARK · FEDERAL · DEARBORN · PLYMOUTH COURT · STATE · WABASH

C53
MANHATTAN BUILDING
431 South Dearborn

C54
OLD COLONY
407 South Dearborn

C55
FISHER BUILDING
343 South Dearborn

C56
CHICAGO BAR ASSOCIATION
321 South Plymouth Court

C57
JOHN MARSHALL LAW
SCHOOL
315 South Plymouth Court

C58
STANDARD CLUB
321 South Dearborn

C59
MONADNOCK BUILDING
53 West Jackson

C60
FEDERAL CENTER
*Adams, Clark, Dearborn
and Jackson*

C61
MARQUETTE BUILDING
140 South Dearborn

C62
BERGHOFF'S
17 West Adams

C63
XEROX CENTER
55 West Monroe

C64
33 WEST MONROE STREET

C65
INLAND STEEL BUILDING
30 West Monroe

C66
FIRST NATIONAL BANK
*Dearborn between Madison
and Monroe*

C67
THREE FIRST NATIONAL
PLAZA
70 West Madison

C68
CONNECTICUT MUTUAL LIFE
33 North Dearborn

C69
BRUNSWICK BUILDING
69 West Washington

C70
RICHARD J. DALEY CENTER
66 West Washington

C71
DELAWARE BUILDING
36 West Randolph

C72
OLIVER BUILDING
159 North Dearborn

C73
THEATER DISTRICT
SELF-PARK
181 North Dearborn

DEARBORN STREET

One of the most important streets in the Central Loop, Dearborn is unique, having much open space and many of the city's most important buildings. The street's character changes as we move from south to north. The blocks south of Jackson have a concentration of early skyscrapers of the 1890s. Moving north, one passes Chicago's three largest plazas, one at the Federal Center, one at the First National Bank, and one at the Richard J. Daley Center. The so-called "theater district" is in the vicinity of Lake and Randolph.

CENTRAL BUSINESS DISTRICT

MANHATTAN BUILDING

OLD COLONY

C53
MANHATTAN BUILDING

431 South Dearborn
William LeBaron Jenney, 1889-91

Completed in the fall of 1891, the Manhattan Building achieved distinction in several ways. It was the first 16-story building ever constructed. Except for the tower of the Auditorium Building, it was the tallest office building in the world. It was the first skyscraper in America to be supported entirely by a metal skeleton, and in addition, it was the first building in America to use portal bracing. It was originally hoped that the Manhattan would be constructed of steel, but because of the cost, cast and wrought iron were used instead. The structure is an early version of a stepped-back building, for the central block is flanked by shorter 9-story wings. This arrangement was to avoid putting too much weight on the party walls to the north and south, which would have caused foundation problems for the adjacent buildings. Jenney also cantilevered the floors along each property line for the same reason. Originally an office building, the Manhattan is now an apartment building.

C54
OLD COLONY

407 South Dearborn
Holabird & Roche, 1894

Construction of the Old Colony was simultaneous with that of the Monadnock addition across the street by the same architects. Both are 17-story, but the Old Colony, with a height of 210 feet, surpassed any of the structures in the south Loop at the time of its construction. The structure is visually in three parts: a three-story base of blue Bedford chiseled stone, an 11-story shaft in cream-colored Roman brick with continuous rising piers, and a three-story Ionic colonnade at the summit. A distinctive feature of the building is its bulbous oriels, which project from the four corners.

C55
FISHER BUILDING

343 South Dearborn
D.H. Burnham & Co., 1896; North addition, Peter J. Weber, 1907

What a contrast the Fisher Building makes with Burnham & Root's original part of the Monadnock Building, completed about five years earlier. Charles B. Atwood, Burnham's designer since Root's death, filled the bays of the Fisher with such expanses of glass that *Inland Architect,* just after its completion, called it "a building literally without walls." The 18-story steel skeleton building is similar in design to the Reliance on State Street, built the previous year. The Fisher, however, stresses verticality to a greater extent; projecting bays rise continuously from the second to the sixteenth stories. The steel skeleton, erected in only about a month, is covered in salmon-colored unglazed terra cotta, molded in the forms of clustered Gothic colonnettes and delicate bands of spandrel moldings. Among the terra cotta details are aquatic animals, alluding to the name of the owner, Lucius Fisher. The north part of the building was added by Peter J. Weber, who had worked for Burnham on the original building.

C56
CHICAGO BAR ASSOCIATION
321 South Plymouth Court
Tigerman/McCurry Architects, 1990

Stanley Tigerman's first design for this building was more obviously in the Gothic style, thought to be appropriate for conservative attorneys, but the design was later trimmed of some of its ornament. Modernized aluminum pinnacles rise above the roof. The structure is a concrete frame with a precast concrete skin and a 38-foot high base of Sardinian granite. Above the entrance is a sculpture by local artist Mary Bloch. The sculpture representis *Justice*, wearing a judge's robe and carrying a dove and orb.

C57
JOHN MARSHALL LAW SCHOOL
315 South Plymouth Court
Pond & Pond, 1911

Originally the City Club, this 3-bay, 6-story building is perhaps Chicago's best example of the work of Irving K. and Allen Pond. The architect brothers, originally from Ann Arbor, Michigan, were important young progressives in Chicago in the early part of the century. Their work, modern in its own right, differs from that of other Chicago school architects. They were influenced more by European architects than by Wright, but like Wright, they emphasized natural materials and textures.

C58
STANDARD CLUB
321 South Dearborn (320 South Plymouth Court)
Albert Kahn, 1926

The reputation of Albert Kahn of Detroit, Michigan was largely built on his reinforced concrete industrial structures. This 10-story building is an historical departure in the Italianate Renaissance style, sheathed in Bedford limestone and pressed brick.

C59
MONADNOCK BUILDING
53 West Jackson
Burnham & Root, 1889-91; Holabird & Roche, 1891-3

The original part of the Monadnock, facing Jackson, has massive brick bearing walls, six feet wide at sidewalk level, and eight feet wide below grade. It must have been truly a startling design when built, for not only was it the tallest structure in the world, but it looked extremely plain to eyes used to very decorative buildings. Root had wanted more ornament, but the owner, Peter Brooks of Boston, interested in a higher return on investment, specified that the design should be strictly functional. The beauty of the structure rests in the proportions and simplicity of its form. The base swells out, expressing stability; the cornice is eliminated and replaced by an outward-flaring, bell-shaped coping, somewhat reminiscent of Egyptian forms. Corners are rounded and gently curving bays alternate with flat portions of wall.

The south addition was built by Shephard Brooks, Peter's brother, who commissioned Holabird & Roche. They employed an all-steel skeleton frame, a three-story base, and pilasters which rise the full height. Although the same height as the earlier structure, the addition has an arcaded 16th story and a 17th story in the attic. Walk through the long marble lobby to observe the restoration of the oak trim, frosted glasswork, and cantilevered ornamental stairs with aluminum railings.

MONADNOCK BUILDING

FEDERAL CENTER

C60
FEDERAL CENTER

Adams, Clark, Dearborn and Jackson
Ludwig Mies van der Rohe, with collaborating architects: Schmidt, Garden & Martin; C.F. Murphy Associates; and A. Epstein & Sons, 1959-74

The Federal Center is a masterful example of Mies' site planning, perfection of relationships, understatement, and attention to detail. Designed in 1959, the complex includes three buildings: the 30-story Everett M. Dirkson Building (1959-64); the 43-story Kluchinski Building (1965-74) and the U.S. Post Office (1966-74). The three structures exhibit a visual continuity by virtue of their pure forms and the repeated use of black painted steel, glass curtain walls, and light gray granite of the lobby walls, floors and exterior pavement. The two office towers have recessed lobbies with glass walls, and continuous steel I-section mullions rising from the second story to the summits of the structures. Contrasting with the rectilinear lines and dark color of the structures is Alexander Calder's brilliant red-painted, 53-foot steel stabile, titled *Flamingo*, which provides a focal point for the plaza. A fourth federal building, named for Ralph Metcalf, has recently been constructed at Clark and Jackson Streets.

C61
MARQUETTE BUILDING

140 South Dearborn
Holabird & Roche, 1894

XEROX CENTER

The design of the 16-story Marquette Building is simple, straightforward, and extremely progressive for its time. Its original owner, Peter Brooks of Boston, with his Chicago agent Owen Aldis, insisted on functionality with maximum light and air. The building is designed with a three-story base and an 11-story shaft, in which the spandrels are recessed behind unbroken piers boldly rising to the summit, which is more ornate. An E-shaped floor plan allows maximum light to every office in the building. The cladding is brown brick and terra cotta. The entrance is marked by large Ionic pilasters of red polished granite, between which are bronze panels by Herman A. MacNeil above the main doorways, showing episodes from Marquette's life. Be sure to visit the small Carrara marble elevator lobby, decorated with mosaics by J.A. Holzer of Tiffany Studios, which illustrate Father Marquette, Joliett, and the Indians.

C62
BERGHOFF'S

17 West Adams
C.M. Palmer, architect of the west building, 1872

Berghoff's Restaurant occupies two adjoining Italianate buildings. The east building is an anonymous, 3-story brick structure with tall narrow arched windows. The building to the west was designed by C.M. Palmer for Potter Palmer, who was responsible for much of the rebuilding of State Street after the great fire. It was recently discovered that this structure has a prefabricated cast iron front, one of only two in the Loop. Panels of iron, cast in the shapes of columns and arches, were bolted onto the structure. The design is similar to Chicago's other cast iron front, the Page Building, at State and Lake.

C63
XEROX CENTER

55 West Monroe
C.F. Murphy Associates, 1980

Helmut Jahn designed this sleek, 40-story, reinforced concrete column-and-slab tower. Sheathing the structure are horizontal bands of white enameled aluminum panels alternating with double-pained silver reflective glass. Jahn readily admits that the design recalls the rounded, polished geometric surfaces of the Art Deco style of the 1920s and 1930s. At the sidewalk level, the exterior lobby walls undulate behind the column line, creating an invitation for the pedestrian to enter. The sparkling white marble lobby is characterized by a crisp geometry as the eye is brought inward along black diagonal banding on the floor and ceiling.

C64
33 WEST MONROE STREET

Skidmore, Owings & Merrill, 1980

This massive, but economical, 28-story steel-frame building is sheathed with rather monotonous gray aluminum panels and insulated glass. The only relief from the blocky form is above the 20th story, from which point every floor is set back, creating a sawtoothed roofline. Within, the architects arranged three atriums, ranging from 5 stories to 10 stories in height. The atriums bring light to interior office spaces, which would otherwise be totally dependent on artificial lighting. The glistening white marble ground-level atrium is dominated by a 70-foot light sculpture by Chryssa. The S.O.M. firm located their own offices here.

C65
INLAND STEEL BUILDING

30 West Monroe
Skidmore, Owings & Merrill, 1957

Bruce Graham, the S.O.M. partner in charge of the Inland Steel design, conceived of the building as two separate units: a 19-story office structure, representing "served" space, and a 25-story service annex, representing "servant" space. The taller annex includes elevators, restrooms, stairs and equipment. The green-tinted curtain wall of the shorter tower reflects its office function, while the windowless steel curtain wall of the taller structure indicates that it is an elevator tower. Fourteen large stainless steel piers stand entirely outside the glass curtain walls which they support, so that no office space is interrupted by the intrusion of a column. The small lobby contains a steel-wire sculpture by Richard Lippold, set in a shallow pool.

C66
FIRST NATIONAL BANK

Dearborn between Madison and Monroe
C.F. Murphy & Associates with The Perkins & Will Partnership, 1964-69

When built, this 850-foot tower was the tallest structure in the Loop. Its flaring form was at once controversial. The parabolic curved shape, however. was a logical solution in response to the bank's need for large clear spaces at ground level and less space on upper office floors. Structurally, the tapered design provides the greatest amount of material near the base, where stress from wind pressure is the greatest. The steel skeleton is sheathed in gray Texas granite. For an almost surreal experience, stand at the base of the north or south facades and look upward. The upsweeping profile of the bank creates a distinctive image on Chicago's skyline. The building's shape functions as the trademark by which it is recognized; its shape becomes an advertisement for the bank itself.

The multi-level plaza, in matching Texas granite, to the south of the bank was designed by landscape architects Novak and Carlson. The plaza has become one of the city's most popular, with its Chagall mosaic, *Les Quatres Saisons*, on a 70-foot long boxcar-shaped wall. The mosaic is protected under a minimalist, bronze-clad canopy designed by Joseph Gonzalez, a partner of Skidmore, Owings & Merrill.

C67
THREE FIRST NATIONAL PLAZA
70 West Madison
Skidmore, Owings & Merrill, 1981

This prismatic structure built on an irregular lot is composed of a 57-story tower, an 11-story unit, and a sloped 9-story atrium connecting the two. A complex saw-toothed effect is created by vertically rising bay windows which alternate with flat wall planes and stepped-back stories in the atrium and at the summit. This was one of the earliest skyscrapers to combine a reinforced concrete core for wind-bracing with a light steel skeleton frame and curtain walls on the periphery. The sheathing is carnelian granite and bronze-tinted glass. Inside the stepped-back, sky-lit lobby with white painted tubular steel space-frame trusses, is a 22-foot bronze sculpture by Henry Moore, entitled *External Internal*.

C68
CONNECTICUT MUTUAL LIFE
33 North Dearborn
Skidmore, Owings & Merrill, 1966

This skeleton frame building has a curtain wall of black polished granite and glass clearly expressing its structure. The building originally had a set-back lobby with an arcade, but this was later enclosed to provide additional street-level commercial space.

C69
BRUNSWICK BUILDING
69 West Washington
Skidmore, Owings & Merrill, 1964

The 36-story Brunswick Building is the product of the collaboration of three S.O.M. partners, Bruce Graham Myron Goldsmith, the structural engineer, Fazlur Khan. It is not the typical skeleton frame, but a monolithic concrete structure with load-bearing walls, one of the first load-bearing skyscrapers since the Monadnock of 1891. The walls resemble Vierendeel trusses, plate girders with regular openings for windows, but instead of metal they are of concrete. The windows increase in size with the building's height. The four walls function as diaphragms joined so integrally that they form a rigid rectangular vertical "tube", highly resistant to wind pressure. An additional tube surrounds the elevator shafts; thus the system is called a "tube-in-a-tube." The walls of the outer tube rest on an enormous windowless ring girder, 24-feet deep. This 9000-ton transfer beam in turn is supported on ten massive, square concrete columns. The innovation of the structural tube made possible the construction of much taller concrete buildings than had been built previously. The columns, pavement, and interior lobby are sheathed in travertine, in contrast to the upper concrete walls, which are painted. On the plaza just west of the Brunswick Building stands the 40-foot sculpture, *Miss Chicago* by Joan Miro, designed in 1967 but not installed and dedicated until 1980.

C70
RICHARD J. DALEY CENTER
66 West Washington
C.F. Murphy & Associates, 1965; Skidmore, Owings & Merrill and Loebl, Schlossman & Bennett, collaborators

As one of the most powerful architectural statements of our century, the Daley Center symbolizes the "big shoulders" of Chicago itself. Nicknamed by the *Chicago Tribune* critic Paul Gapp as "Chicago's Rambo," the structure expresses its bold form with utmost clarity. Chief architect on the project was Jacques Brownson, a highly talented former student of Mies van der Rohe. A determinant in the design was the requirement for large lobbies and courtrooms, and high ceilings; hence, the necessity to have a minimum number of columns and a maximum ceiling height. Brownson created 87-foot spans—the longest in any skyscraper of such size in the world at the time. Massive cruciform piers carry 6-foot deep trusses and plate girder spandrels. For its 31 stories, the building has a total height of 648 feet. Many of the 120 courtrooms are 2-story with 26-foot ceilings.

The cladding with its brown patina is Cor-ten, a steel alloy which rusts initially but then stabilizes, forming a dark brown corrosion-resistant coating. Thus, painting the steel, which is a constant maintenance for most steel clad buildings, is not required. Cor-ten was also adopted for the 50-foot sculpture, representing the head of a woman, by Picasso, erected on the plaza and complementing the building. The Daley Center, with its vigor and power, is truly one of the gems of the city.

C71
DELAWARE BUILDING
36 West Randolph
Wheelock & Thomas, 1874; Two stories added by Holabird & Roche,1889

One of Chicago's few extant buildings of the immediate post-fire era, the Delaware has been carefully renovated at a cost of over $2 million. Originally called the Bryant Building, it was later called the Real Estate Board Building. It is an excellent example of the Italianate style, with arched and rectangular windows of tall proportions and an ornate bracketed cornice. The two upper stories, added by Holabird & Roche in 1889, have a circular corner bay in contrast to the polygonal bays of the older structure. Be sure to enter the small lobby and go to the second floor, where you enter a sky-lit atrium surrounded by balconies. Delightful patterns of light are created by round glass block insertions in the iron floors and stairs. The galleried arrangement was extremely common in late nineteenth century office buildings.

C72
OLIVER BUILDING
159 North Dearborn
Holabird & Roche, 1907-08

The Oliver Company manufactured typewriters, images of which can be seen in the cast iron spandrels of the facade. If, however, one looks past the ornament, the massing is typical of the Chicago style, and especially characteristic of that of Holabird & Roche, in whose work the expression of structure is dominant.

C73
THEATER DISTRICT SELF-PARK
181 North Dearborn
Hammond, Beeby & Babka, Inc., 1987

Repetitious arches and projecting marquee-style canopies relate this parking garage visually to the traditional architecture of nearby theaters.

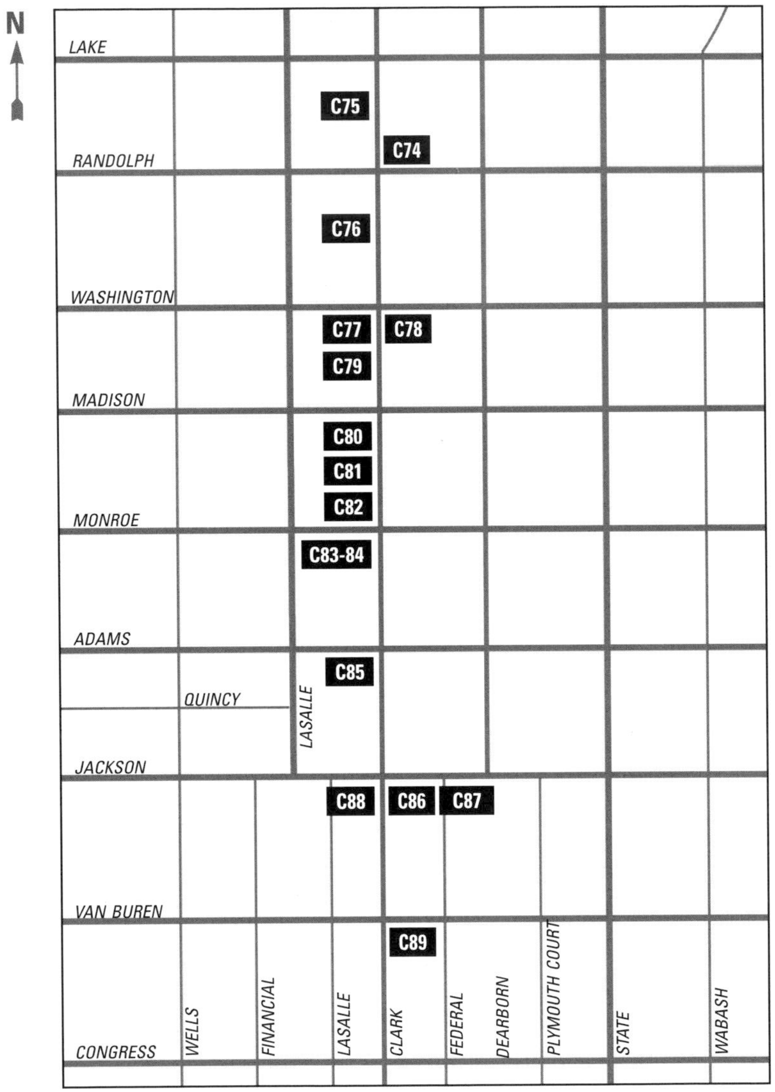
N
LAKE
RANDOLPH
WASHINGTON
MADISON
MONROE
ADAMS
QUINCY
JACKSON
VAN BUREN
CONGRESS
WELLS
FINANCIAL
LASALLE
CLARK
FEDERAL
DEARBORN
PLYMOUTH COURT
STATE
WABASH
C74
C75
C76
C77
C78
C79
C80
C81
C82
C83-84
C85
C86
C87
C88
C89

C74
CHICAGO TITLE AND TRUST CENTER
161-171 North Clark

C75
JAMES R. THOMPSON CENTER
100 West Randolph

C76
COUNTY BUILDING AND CITY HALL
118 North Clark

C77
CONWAY BUILDING
111 West Washington

C78
CHICAGO TEMPLE
31 North Clark

C79
AVONDALE CENTER
20 North Clark

C80
CHICAGO LOOP SYNAGOGUE
16 South Clark

C81
TWO FIRST NATIONAL PLAZA
20 South Clark

C82
40 SOUTH CLARK BUILDING
100 West Monroe Building

C83
HARRIS TRUST AND SAVINGS BANK
111 West Monroe

C84
HARRIS TRUST AND SAVINGS BANK ADDITION
Southwest corner of Clark and Monroe

C85
BANKERS BUILDING
105 West Adams

C86
RALPH METCALF BUILDING
77 West Jackson

C87
UNION LEAGUE CLUB
65 West Jackson

C88
TRANS-UNION BUILDING
111 West Jackson

C89
METROPOLITAN CORRECTIONAL CENTER
71 West Van Buren

CLARK STREET

From 1835, when Chicago's first city hall and county building was erected on Clark between Randolph and Washington, the street was established as a government center. Today the street boasts city, county, state and federal buildings, including the present City Hall and County Building on the same spot as the original, the James Thompson Center, the State of Illinois Building, the Richard J. Daley Center, and as part of the Federal Center, the U.S. Post Office and the Metcalf Building.

C74
CHICAGO TITLE AND TRUST CENTER
161-171 North Clark
Kohn Pedersen Fox, 1992

This 50-story structure is composed of a 13-story base, which matches the height of the City Hall-County Building diagonally across the street, on which are surmounted two massive towers, one much taller than the other. The structure is sheathed in "Maurredu" white granite from Sardinia with aluminum spandrels and mullions.

C75
JAMES R. THOMPSON CENTER
100 West Randolph
Murphy/Jahn, 1985

Helmet Jahn designed this dramatic and controversial, 17-story truncated glass cylinder, looking more like a spaceship than a government building. Its surface of alternating opaque and reflective glass in blue, gray and white obstructs any sense of scale. Harry Weese has called it "tinselly and decadent...a goldfish bowl that symbolizes the fragility of our time," while Paul Gapp of the *Chicago Tribune* described it as "light, lacy, intricate...the most visually startling building to be constructed in the Loop since the skyscraper was invented here in 1883." Governor Jim Thompson, who commissioned the structure, called it "the first building of the 21st century."

The entrance is on a rounded sloping facade oriented toward the corner of Randolph and Clark Streets. Be sure to enter the structure to experience a powerful and dramatic space: seventeen open stories beneath a 160-foot cylindrical dome. The sculpture in front of the building is Jean Dubuffet's large *Monument with Standing Beast.*

C76
COUNTY BUILDING AND CITY HALL
118 North Clark
Holabird & Roche, 1907

The impressive neoclassical granite facades of the County Building have a four-story base surmounted by a six-story colonnade of gigantic proportions: columns are 96 feet high and 8 feet in diameter. Two buildings in one, the city and county building fill the block between Clark, LaSalle, Washington and Randolph. The County Building, facing Clark Street, was constructed first; completion of City Hall was four years later. Inside a magnificent Renaissance style corridor with elliptical mosaic-covered vaults connects the Clark and LaSalle Street entrances.

RICHARD J. DALEY CENTER
66 West Washington
C.F. Murphy & Associates, 1965
See Dearborn Street Tour, C69

C77
CONWAY BUILDING
111 West Washington
D.H. Burnham & Co., 1913

Architecturally speaking, the 21-story Conway Building is not one of Burnham's better structures. Typical of some of his other late works, it is loaded with excessive ornament. The terra cotta is an inexpensive facing material easy to mold in repetitive patterns. For many years this was the Chicago Title and Trust Building.

C78
CHICAGO TEMPLE
31 North Clark (77 West Washington)
Holabird & Roche, 1923

The Methodist Church, which still owns this building, combined a 21-story office building with an eight-story spire containing a 3-story parsonage and a 1500-seat sanctuary. The Clark Street entrance leads to the church, while the principal office entrance is on Washington. Because of the building's religious function, the Gothic style seems appropriate. The limestone facades are adorned with clustered colonnettes, sprockets, pinnacles, and gargoyles, borrowed from French medieval architecture. The spire, at 556 feet high, made the structure the tallest in Chicago when built, and it remains today the tallest church in the world.

C79
AVONDALE CENTER
20 North Clark
A. Epstein & Sons, 1980

The piers of this restrained, 36-story tower are concealed behind a curtain wall of red Aswan flame-cut granite, bronze anodized aluminum, and dark tinted glass. In the lobby is a sculpture by Agam.

C80
CHICAGO LOOP SYNAGOGUE
16 South Clark
Loebl, Schlossman & Bennett, 1957

A wall of stained glass by Abraham Rattner, entitled *Let there be Light*, sheathes the facade of this narrow synagogue tucked between larger buildings. A metal sculpture, *The Hands of Peace,* forms a cantilevered awning over the entrance and provides a focus for the design.

C81
TWO FIRST NATIONAL PLAZA
20 South Clark
C.F. Murphy & Associates and The Perkins & Will Partnership, 1972

This 30-story annex to the First National Bank, built by the same architects, has a structure which more clearly expresses its steel skeleton than does the main bank. The annex is sheathed with gigantic dark brown U-formed plate steel panels, each one bay wide and one story high. Where panels meet one another, reveals are formed which visually enhance the grid-like design. While this structure is much in the same tradition as the Daley Center and the CNA Center, both Murphy buildings, the spandrels and columns here are in the same plane, giving the structure a flatter appearance than the earlier buildings.

C82
40 SOUTH CLARK BUILDING
(100 West Monroe Building)
Frank D. Chase, 1927

This 22-story building is simpler than most of the Art Deco period.

C83
HARRIS TRUST AND SAVINGS BANK
111 West Monroe
Shepley, Rutan & Coolidge, 1911

One of the most beautiful facades in the city, this 20-story Renaissance revival bank was created by the Boston firm which gave Chicago the Art Institute and the Cultural Center (formerly the public library). Most impressive is its 5-story, variegated red polished granite base with immense full-rounded Ionic columns. The red brick facade above is dominated by tall arched window openings with pleasing proportions. The bank is sandwiched between its two additions, one facing Clark Street and one on LaSalle.

C84
HARRIS TRUST AND SAVINGS BANK ADDITION
Southwest corner of Clark and Monroe
Skidmore Owings & Merrill, 1960

Stainless steel piers rise from the sidewalk to the summit, while stainless steel mullions alternating with tinted glass, sheathing the walls above the set-back lobby.

BANK OF AMERICA BUILDING
(Originally the Field Building)
230 South Clark (231 South LaSalle)
Graham, Anderson, Probst & White,1932
See LaSalle Street Tour, C106

C85
BANKERS BUILDING
105 West Adams
Burnham Brothers, 1927

The massing of this 4l-story tower is typical of architecture of the late 1920s: a tall central unit is flanked by shorter blocks on either side. A terra cotta base with panels of floral ornaments is surmounted by brick walls.

C86
RALPH METCALF BUILDING
77 West Jackson
Fujikawa, Johnson & Associates, 1992

The full block along Clark Street between Jackson and Van Buren is occupied by the new federal building, which bears a visual relationship to two other federal buildings, the Dirkson and Kluczynski, nearby on Jackson Street. The architects, both of whom had worked in the Mies van der Rohe firm at the time he was designing the Federal Center, are known for their Miesian-style buildings. Here the steel skeleton is clad in dark gray thermal-finished granite, as opposed to black-painted steel in the earlier buildings. All of these buildings have an understated elegance. Joseph Fujikawa claimed, "Federal buildings should show restraint and present a dignified image." (*Inland Architect*, March/April, 1989, p.20)

C87
UNION LEAGUE CLUB
65 West Jackson
Mundie & Jensen, 1928

Between the Monadnock Building and the Metcalf Building is this 22-story Italian Renaissance style tower, built by two architects who were former partners of William LeBaron Jenney. Notice the palazzo arrangement: a 4-story, limestone base, surmounted by a series of very tall arched windows, with an additional row of arched windows near the top. The previous Union League Club, which had been constructed on the same site by Jenney in 1886, was demolished in 1927. Many of the Chicago School architects were members around the turn-of-the-century: Adler, Sullivan, Beman, Burnham, Root, Graham, Jenney, Mundie, Marshall, and others.

C88
TRANS-UNION BUILDING
111 West Jackson
A. Epstein & Sons, 1961

This 24-story structure, built for the Union Tank Car Company, has a reinforced concrete frame with projecting piers, and glass infill.

C89
METROPOLITAN CORRECTIONAL CENTER
71 West Van Buren
Harry Weese & Associates, 1975

Harry Weese gave a dramatic triangular form to this jail for detainees awaiting trial or serving short sentences. The shape is visually exciting because of its contrast to the buildings around it, and the building is non-threatening to its neighbors because it doesn't look like a jail. Structurally, the 27-story tower is of poured-in-place, flat-plate concrete. The concrete exterior walls are marked with horizontal grooves indicating floor levels. Between these, floor-to-ceiling slit-windows only five inches wide seem to be randomly scattered. Every cell has one of these narrow, bar-less windows, as well as a toilet, carpet and storage space. The cells are arranged in groups around a brightly-painted, two-story core multi-purpose room. An exercise court is on the roof. In 1977 the building won a national AIA award.

RALPH METCALF BUILDING

METROPOLITAN CORRECTIONAL CENTER

N

LAKE

RANDOLPH

WASHINGTON

MADISON

MONROE

ADAMS

JACKSON

VAN BUREN

CONGRESS

CHICAGO RIVER

LASALLE

QUINCY

WACKER DRIVE

FRANKLIN · WELLS · FINANCIAL · LASALLE · CLARK · FEDERAL

C91 C90
C92
C93
C94
C95 C96
C97 C98
C99 C100
C101
C102
C104 C103
C105
C107 C106
C108
C110 C109
C111
C112

C90
203 NORTH LASALLE

C91
200 NORTH LASALLE

C92
HEITMAN CENTER
180 North Lasalle

C93
STATE OF ILLINOIS BUILDING
160 North LaSalle

C94
120 NORTH LASALLE

C95
30 NORTH LASALLE

C96
AMERICAN NATIONAL BANK
& TRUST BUILDING
33 North LaSalle

C97
TWO NORTH LASALLE

C98
ONE NORTH LASALLE

C99
10 SOUTH LASALLE

C100
ELEVEN SOUTH LASALLE

C101
NORTHERN TRUST BANK
50 South LaSalle

C102
HARRIS TRUST AND SAVINGS
BANK ADDITION
115 South LaSalle

C103
LASALLE BANK
135 South LaSalle

C104
190 SOUTH LASALLE

C105
THE ROOKERY
209 South LaSalle

C106
BANK OF AMERICA BUILDING
231 South LaSalle

C107
FEDERAL RESERVE BANK
230 South LaSalle

C108
CHICAGO BOARD OF TRADE
141 West Jackson

C109
TRADERS BUILDING
401 South LaSalle

C110
CHICAGO BOARD OF OPTIONS
EXCHANGE
400 South LaSalle

C111
ONE FINANCIAL PLACE
440 South LaSalle

C112
MIDWEST STOCK EXCHANGE
440 South LaSalle

LASALLE STREET

The financial district of Chicago, LaSalle Street is architecturally dominated by classical porticoes typical of banking structures, interspersed by other contrasting and highly interesting structures. The sidewalks are crowded with rapidly moving pedestrians—bankers, stock brokers, lawyers entering and leaving these structures. The office buildings crowd each other, forming a darkened canyon, difficult for the sun to penetrate. The architecture contributes to the excitement of the street, which, moving southward, terminates and climaxes dramatically at the Board of Trade. The street continues again at Van Buren with the Chicago Board of Options Exchange, One Financial Place and the Midwest Stock Exchange.

CENTRAL BUSINESS DISTRICT

203 NORTH LASALLE

C90
203 NORTH LASALLE
Skidmore, Owings & Merrill, 1985

Originally called the Transportation Building, the structure was designed by Skidmore partner Adrian Smith to provide easy transfer between automobile, train and plane. It incorporates a direct entrance to the subway, houses a number of airline offices, and includes a ten-story parking garage in which every level features a different color and a tune relating to a different city. The upper office floors are wrapped around a multi-story atrium on the east and a smaller atrium on the west. A large-scale lobby, featuring chrome, black and green marble, and the curvilinear shapes of the Art Deco, spans the width of the structure from LaSalle Street to Clark.

C91
200 NORTH LASALLE
Perkins & Will Partnership, 1984

An unusual effect is achieved by the staggered planes of the facades of this 30-story office tower. The serrated plan was conceived by the firm's designer, Wojciech Madeyski, in order to create ten corner windows per floor, thereby providing more expensive and desirable offices. The entirely glass curtain wall is half clear, while the rest was sprayed white on the back side to appear pale green. Madeyski explained, "The idea was to create a building that would appear translucent," like an extruded ice cube." The entrance lobby is a four-story atrium, set back from Lake Street, and facing east.

C92
HEITMAN CENTER
180 North LaSalle
Harry Weese Associates, 1972

This 38-story reinforced concrete frame structure has an unusually bold form, attractive in its proportions. Economical because no cladding material was employed, the bare concrete is now painted a dark purplish-brown. The brick-paved plaza with trees is a welcome relief in the Loop where few open spaces exist.

C93
STATE OF ILLINOIS BUILDING
160 North LaSalle
Burnham Brothers, 1924
Renovation, Holabird & Root, 1991

Two sons of Daniel Burnham designed this 20-story, U-shaped structure, originally known as the Burnham Building. It was purchased by the State of Illinois in 1946 and is still used by the state, in addition to the James R. Thompson Center nearby. In the recent remodeling by Holabird & Root, a towering glass curtain-wall atrium with a series of set-backs was created in the court of the U-plan.

C94
120 NORTH LASALLE
120 North LaSalle
Murphy/Jahn, 1991

In many ways one of the most distinctive buildings in the Loop, the architect Helmut Jahn was faced with a difficult design problem: to create a large, narrow structure with strong visibility on a mid-block narrow lot. The building's striking shapes are unconventional and border on Deconstructivism. The arch shape at the summit abuts into a wall; a subtle bay juts forward from the LaSalle facade and then cuts back; shapes are fragmented. On the other hand, the tower is a functional, viable and beautiful form. One of its most unusual design features is the scalloped effect in the gray granite base wall. Another is the "ladder" feature, which is a sort of three-dimensional pattern in stone running horizontally along the north wall wrapping the structure, moving up and over the entrance and finally running vertically to the summit. The primary focal point is the outwardly-arched wall over the entrance, on which is a brilliant blue and gold mosaic of *Daedalus and Icarus* by Roger Brown. Parking is provided within the structure, with access on the Wells Street side.

C95
30 NORTH LASALLE
Thomas E. Stanley of Dallas, Texas, 1975

Adler & Sullivan's old Chicago Stock Exchange, which formerly stood on this site, became economically unfeasible by the 1970s; it was demolished in spite of loud protests from preservationists. This functional, speculative office tower replaced it. The base is dark bluish black granite, and the piers are faced with black grooved aluminum sheathing.

C96
AMERICAN NATIONAL BANK & TRUST BUILDING
33 North LaSalle
Graham, Anderson, Probst & White, 1929-30

In construction at the time of the 1929 stock market crash, the building has a granite base, limestone-clad superstructure and recessed bronze spandrels. The lobby elevator doors with tree-of-plenty designs are some of the city's best examples of the Art Deco style.

C97
TWO NORTH LASALLE
Perkins & Will Partnership, 1979

This highly functional, 27-story office tower is a vertical box with rounded corners, occupying the full site. It is constructed of concrete columns and flat plate floor slabs and sheathed with horizontal bands of light gray aluminum sandwich panels, alternating with ribbon windows of dark gray glass.

C98
ONE NORTH LASALLE
Vitzhum & Burns, 1930

This 49-story building was constructed on the site of the old Tacoma Building, a significant early skyscraper by Holabird & Roche. Today both One North LaSalle and the structure to the north are occupied by the American National Bank. Both structures are stepped-back Art Deco works, completed in 1930. The original Art Deco lobby is intact.

120 NORTH LASALLE

C99
10 SOUTH LASALLE
Otis Building base by Holabird & Roche, 1909; Moriyama & Teshima Planners Ltd. of Toronto with Holabird & Root, 1987

Only the 4-story shell of a granite and terra cotta base remains from old Otis Building, which stood on this site since 1909. The 37-story newer steel skeletal structure is clad, from the fifth story up in blue-painted aluminum with infill of silvery blue tinted glass and with large tubular green moldings, somewhat incongruous with the Corinthian-style details of the older base. As if the colors weren't contrast enough, the architects scooped out a semicircular recess up to the seventh story above the entrance.

C100
ELEVEN SOUTH LASALLE
(Originally the Lumber Exchange)
Holabird & Roche, 1915; Renovation: Hammond, Beeby & Babka, 1983

The upper facade of the 16-story, former Lumber Exchange Building is of dark terra cotta with ornate Italianate designs. Hammond, Beeby & Babka gave the structure greater visibility with a strongly classical entrance and lobby. Set within a green marble base, they set a bold, simplified Palladian entrance in contrasting white variegated and black marble. The small lobby is a gem with its vaulted ceiling and marble walls.

C101
NORTHERN TRUST BANK
50 South LaSalle
Frost & Granger, 1906; Frost & Henderson, 1928-30; C.F. Murphy Associates, 1967

The Northern Trust, in the Renaissance palazzo style, has two-story engaged Ionic columns and a frieze of triglyphs and metopes, an unusual combination of two distinct classical orders. The base has a much heavier look, with grills at the windows; the main level has balustrades with large arched windows, and bracket-like keystones above the arches. Built originally as a four-story structure, additional stories were added in 1930 and 1967.

C102
HARRIS TRUST AND SAVINGS BANK ADDITION
115 South LaSalle
Skidmore, Owings & Merrill, 1975-77

A powerful structure, this 38-story bank addition boldly expresses its skeleton structure, and in that respect is especially characteristic of the architecture of Chicago. The designer was Bruce Graham, a former student of Mies van der Rohe. Related in design to the Daley Center, the building has extremely wide bays and cruciform piers. In each building, the facades have three bays. In the Harris Trust Building, the piers are 45 feet apart and clad in stainless steel. A bronze fountain sculpture by Russel Secrest adorns the granite plaza.

C103
LASALLE BANK

135 South LaSalle
Graham, Anderson, Probst & White, 1928-1934

This magnificent example of the streamlined Art Deco style stands on the site of the world's first skyscraper, the Home Insurance Building of 1885. The present building was originally owned by the Marshall Field family and hence, for many years was called the Field Building. The windows are arranged in regular vertical bands, recessed from unbroken limestone-clad piers, emphasizing the height of the 43-story central tower with its 23-story corner wings. The simple bold shapes with flat undecorated roof give the structure a more modern appearance than other buildings of its time, perhaps because some restraint was required during the depression. The block-long lobby connecting the Clark and LaSalle entrances is Art Deco with cream-colored marble walls and fluted piers, stainless steel bridges connecting balconies at the mezzanine level, and elegant elevator doors.

C104
190 SOUTH LASALLE

John Burgee Architects with Philip Johnson, 1986

Philip Johnson, who made his reputation forty years ago as an International Style architect, has made an about-face in recent years to champion the cause of Post-Modernism. In this structure, Johnson pays homage to the first great Chicago School style, in particular to the Masonic Temple, built by Burnham & Root in 1892 with two sharply pointed gables facing the front.

Johnson's 42-story tower is Cyclopian in scale. The 5-story, 68-foot, flame-cut red Spanish granite base has a 50-foot high entrance and immense lighting sconces and hardware. Surmounting the base, the facade walls are pink granite, the whole topped with bronze gable roofs. The lobby is one of Chicago's most magnificent interiors with walls of red polished Alicante marble, a floor of black and white Botticino marble, and a 55-foot high groin vaulted ceiling is covered with actual gold leaf.

C105
THE ROOKERY

209 South LaSalle
Burnham & Root, 1885-88

Once the tallest structure in Chicago, the 11-story Rookery stands as one of Chicago's most excellent and unusual landmark structures. Named after a water tower previously on the site, a roosting place for birds, the building has attracted attention since it opened. It provides a visual feast of complex details, a variety of surface texture and warm red earth tones. The base of the structure is of red rough-hewn granite with a polished red granite colonnade alternating with display windows, while the walls above are of red pressed brick ornamented with terra cotta. One's eye is directed toward the broad arched entrance surrounded by elaborate Romanesque carving, including roosting birds and elaborate patterns with a Near Eastern flavor. At the summit, turrets rise fortress-like from the central bays as well as from the corners. One of Chicago's most beautiful interiors is the Rookery's two-story light-filled court, full of white marble with lacy patterns in gold leaf, the result of a 1905 remodeling by Frank Lloyd Wright.

C106
BANK OF AMERICA BUILDING
231 South LaSalle
Graham, Anderson, Probst & White 1923-24; Remodeling, Skidmore, Owings & Merrill, 1981 and 1990

Formerly Continental Bank the building is a 19-story, Roman revival structure of gray limestone with a grand Ionic colonnade at its entrance. Its pediment features a large eagle in the center with acroterion sculpture at the corners and the peak. Inside on the second floor is the main banking hall, an immense room in the form of a Roman basilica surrounded by 28 tall Ionic fluted columns. Above is a Roman style gilded coffered ceiling and a wide frieze of allegorical paintings by Jules Guerin.

C107
FEDERAL RESERVE BANK
230 South LaSalle
Graham, Anderson, Probst & White, 1922; Addition, Naess & Murphy, 1957; Addition, Holabird & Root, 1986

A grand 3-story portico with six Corinthian columns supporting an entablature and pediment projects and forms the entrance to this stately banking building. Light gray limestone cladding relates the structure to the Continental Bank and other buildings on the street. The magnificent temple-like lobby at the mezzanine level, has been restored, although with some changes. The floor was removed in 1986, thus creating a street-level 4-story lobby. The original neoclassical ceiling was restored with gold leaf and chandeliers.

C108
CHICAGO BOARD OF TRADE
141 West Jackson
Holabird & Root, 1929-30; Additions: Murphy/Jahn, 1983; Fujikawa, Johnson & Associates, 1997

The Board of Trade sits dramatically at the foot of LaSalle Street, a focal point framed by the canyon-like walls of financial institutions on either side of the street. Its 45 stories rise in stages narrowing toward its summit. Above the entrance, a large clock is flanked by relief carvings of two hooded figures, one of Osiris with a sheaf of wheat and the other, an Indian holding a stalk of corn. Capping the structure is a pyramidal roof, crowned with a 32-foot aluminum sculpture of *Ceres*, the goddess of agriculture, by sculptor John Storrs, and an appropriate symbol for commodities exchanged on the Board of Trade. The 3-story lobby is a masterpiece in the streamlined Art Deco style with eleven varieties of marble. Black marble piers and buff-colored cascading shapes frame the balconied elevator lobby.

The addition by Helmut Jahn is a 23-story, glass curtain wall structure with a pyramidal roof topped by a finial based on the octagonal Board of Trade logo. The 2-story trading room on the fourth floor of this annex is column-free space 128 feet wide. The weight of the upper stories is carried on eight 128-foot long trusses. On the twelfth floor is an open atrium with offices arranged in a U-shaped plan backing up against the limestone exterior wall of the older building. In numerous ways Jahn reinterpreted the Art Deco elements of the older building in the new atrium, entrances and hallways. He repeated the scalloped "inverted waterfall" shapes of the original lobby in the wall surfaces, floor patterns, lighting fixtures, furniture, elevators and the teal green Van Buren entrance to the annex.

The most recent addition by Fujikawa, Johnson & Associates is a monolithic, four-story structure, visible from Clark Street. Inside is a two-story vestibule in the shape of an elongated octagon of elegant proportions and a trading room, which is an immense column-free space built on a concrete waffle slab capable of supporting great weight.

CHICAGO BOARD OF TRADE

C109
TRADERS BUILDING

401 South LaSalle

Holabird and Roche, 1914; Renovation, Booth/Hansen & Associates, 1984

This 17-story red brick and terra cotta tower was built as the Fort Dearborn Hotel. Booth/Hansen restored the exterior, created a 17-story atrium surrounded on three sides by offices, and constructed a new lobby of mahogany and marble, based in part on the restrained and tasteful design of the original.

C110
CHICAGO BOARD OF OPTIONS EXCHANGE

400 South LaSalle

Skidmore, Owings & Merrill, 1983

The Chicago Board of Options Exchange, along with One Financial Place, the Midwest Stock Exchange and a small park, comprise One Financial Center. The three structures, all designed by Bruce Graham of Skidmore, Owings & Merrill, are visually connected by their cladding of Imperial red granite. The CBOE, the largest options exchange in the world, is a seven-story structure with a 44,000 square foot trading room. Connecting One Financial Center with the Board of Trade, is a glass-enclosed, steel bridge at the fourth-story level, cantilevered on a giant pier where it meets the Board of Trade.

C111
ONE FINANCIAL PLACE

440 South LaSalle

Skidmore, Owings & Merrill, 1985

One Financial Place was the most expensive office building in Chicago when built. Bruce Graham designed this 40-story, chamfer-cornered tube with forty continuous vertical bays. The exterior bearing walls are sheathed in Imperial red granite quarried in Sweden and finished in Italy. The windows are of gray tinted insulated glass. A two-story lobby, which serves as a concourse between the other two buildings, is finished in Italian Brescia marble and Imperial red granite. On the west, the lobby faces one of Chicago's most successful plazas, a block-long landscaped area with a fountain and reflecting pool and a stunning sculpture of a horse, *San Marco II*, by Venetian artist Ludovico de Luigi.

C112
MIDWEST STOCK EXCHANGE

440 South LaSalle

Skidmore, Owings & Merrill, 1985

Spanning the Congress Expressway and adjoining One Financial Place to the south is this 6-story structure, which has a 19,000 square foot trading room. Most conspicuous in the design are the two large glazed arches on the east and west facades overlooking the Congress Expressway. The shapes are reminiscent of Louis Sullivan's broad arches, but here they are only skin deep as part of the curtain wall hanging from the steel frame. The cost was controversial, at $450,000 per window. Behind the windows are a sports club and restaurant.

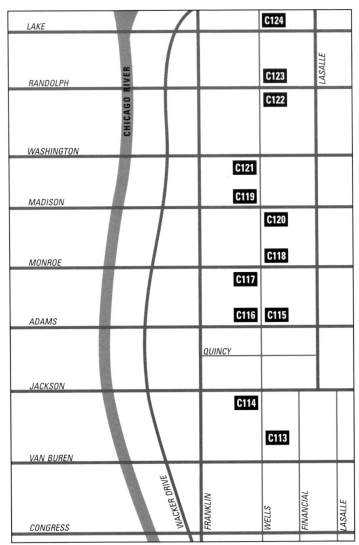

C113
INSURANCE EXCHANGE
175 West Jackson

C114
MCKINLOCK BUILDING
209 West Jackson

C115
MIDLAND HOTEL
176 West Adams

C116
200 WEST ADAMS

C117
WILLIAMS BUILDING
205 West Monroe

C118
NORTHERN TRUST BUILDING
AND PARK
*Northeast Corner of Monroe
and Wells*

C119
MADISON PLAZA
200 West Madison

C120
181 WEST MADISON

C121
WASHINGTON BLOCK
40 North Wells

C122
BISMARCK HOTEL
171 West Randolph

C123
RANDOLPH TOWER
188 West Randolph

C124
TRUSTEES SYSTEMS SERVICE
BUILDING
201 North Wells

WELLS STREET

From Congress to Lake Street

Wells, Franklin and South Wacker were once the heart of the garment district. Since Wells has undergone fewer transformations than its neighbor streets to the west, it retains a glimmer of the atmosphere of the last century. Along with structures for light manufacturing were office buildings and newspaper headquarters. With the most recent structures at Madison Street, Wells has become quite visually diverse.

WILLIAMS BUILDING

C113
INSURANCE EXCHANGE
175 West Jackson
D.H. Burnham & Co., 1912; Addition to south,
Graham, Anderson, Probst & White, 1928

Fronting on Jackson, Van Buren and Wells, the
Insurance Exchange is typical of many of Burnham's
early 20th-century buildings. Ornamented with Ionic
columns and pilasters and various classical detailing,
the surfaces are covered in white glazed terra cotta.
The facades terminate in a double-story, continuous
colonnade at the top.

C114
MCKINLOCK BUILDING
209 West Jackson
Charles S. Frost, 1898

This late 19th century structure in warm tones of red
granite and red brick is progressive in its rectilinearity
and open form, in spite of its classical detailing popular in its time. The eleventh and twelfth stories were
added in 1918. The more recent street-level remodeling is in contradiction to the character of the original
building.

C115
MIDLAND HOTEL
176 West Adams
Karl M. Vitzhum, 1927

Between Wells and LaSalle, this 22-story hotel main-
tains some of its original character. The lobby has
Renaissance-style reliefs and a gilded ceiling.

C116
200 WEST ADAMS
Fujikawa, Johnson & Associates, 1985

Aluminum and blue-tinted reflective glass sheathe this
30-story structure. The building was one of the first in
Chicago to combine a reinforced concrete tubular
core with steel framing, a system which developed
largely to save construction time. The core could be
poured while the steel was being fabricated and
shipped. The strength of the concrete also made possible the reduction of the size of the steel members,
and therefore a reduction in cost.

C117
WILLIAMS BUILDING
205 West Monroe
Holabird & Roche, 1898

This beautiful ten-story building combines red terra
cotta on the ground level with molded red brick above.
Uniformly-paired openings in the facades are
recessed behind prominent continuous piers. The
building's form is simple and geometric, yet organic,
relating it to the work of Louis Sullivan and the early
Prairie School, just beginning to take shape. Overlaid
on this structure, and in fact emphasizing it, are classical details of exquisite quality: dentil patterns under
the windows, egg-and-dart and dentils forming borders at the cornice and elsewhere, and pilasters flanking the entrance.

C118
NORTHERN TRUST BUILDING AND PARK
Northeast Corner of Monroe and Wells
C.F. Murphy Associates, 1967

The west addition to the Northern Trust Building, a
strongly vertical structure with rough granite piers and
recessed spandrels, opens onto a small but beautifully
landscaped serene plaza with greenery and gray brick
retaining walls.

C119
MADISON PLAZA
200 West Madison
Skidmore, Owings & Merrill, 1982

Bruce Graham was the designer of this 45-story office tower, in which the two wings are joined by a saw-toothed facade, resulting in a plan with eight corner offices per floor. The curtain wall, which alternates wide bands of polished granite with narrow bands of reflective glass, produces a highly energy-efficient structure. The roof is set back at the 39th and 44th floors. The visual focus, dominating the building's small corner plaza, is Louise Nevelson's steel sculpture, *Dawn Shadows,* supposedly inspired by the elevated tracks.

C120
181 WEST MADISON
Cesar Pelli, 1990

Chicago's only building by Argentine-born Cesar Pelli was inspired by Eliel Saarinen's second-prize design for the Tribune Tower. Like Saarinen's 1922 design, the structure has a strong blocky effect with a series of set-backs near the summit and paired windows recessed between closely-spaced, upwardly-sweeping piers. This 50-story tower, sheathed in flame-cut pearl granite, glistens with metallic accented mullions and nickel-plated finials. On the sidewalk level, a five-story glass-roofed loggia protects pedestrians from the elements and provides an inviting entrance into the lobby surrounded by shops and restaurants and adorned by two wall sculptures by Frank Stella.

C121
WASHINGTON BLOCK
40 North Wells
Frederick and Edward Baumann, 1873

A rare surviving example of the Baumanns' work is this Italianate office building. Its sandstone facades are deeply carved with classical and Victorian details, including lion's heads and floral and foliage motifs. The interior still retains a spiral staircase and marble fireplaces. Frederick Bauman's influential book, *A Theory of Isolated Pier Foundations*, written in the same year that the Washington Block was built, was influential on the development of the early skyscrapers, since the higher buildings were entirely dependent on the adequacy of their foundations.

C122
BISMARCK HOTEL
171 West Randolph
Rapp & Rapp, 1926

The 16-story hotel is combined with a 22-story office building, extending between Wells Street and LaSalle.

C123
RANDOLPH TOWER
(Formerly the Stuben Club Building)
188 West Randolph
Vitzhum & Burns, 1929

This office structure, which has 27 stories with a 15-story, octagonal tower, is typical of the commercial architecture of its time.

C124
TRUSTEES SYSTEMS SERVICE BUILDING
201 North Wells
Thielbar & Fugard, 1930

Representative of the best modernist work of Thielbar & Fugard, this 28-story ziggurat tower has a strong, clearly-expressed vertical emphasis through its repetitious unbroken mullions. The structural system is unusual with cast iron columns embedded inside spiral concrete ones.

181 WEST MADISON

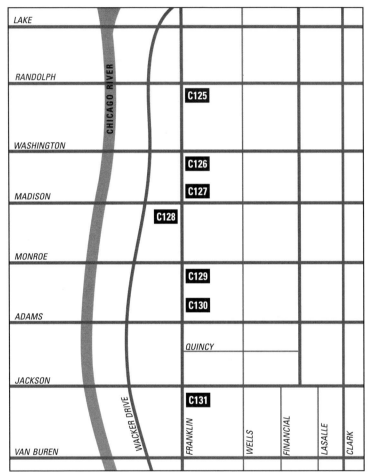

N

C125
ILLINOIS BELL
TELEPHONE BUILDING
225 West Randolph

C126
225 WEST WASHINGTON

C127
ONE NORTH FRANKLIN

C128
303 WEST MADISON

C129
AT&T
100 South Franklin

C130
USG BUILDING
125 South Franklin

C131
BROOKS BUILDING
223 West Jackson

FRANKLIN STREET

From Randolph to Jackson

Once the heart of the garment district, Franklin Street was lined with wholesale stores, warehouses, and small factories called "sweatshops". Over the years, the street's image declined as businesses pulled out or deteriorated, and its older buildings became less desirable. In recent years, however, the street has become revitalized. Developers, who no longer were able to find building sites on Wacker or Lasalle, sought nearby property. Because of number of new buildings now, the street has become a desirable office location.

ONE NORTH FRANKLIN

C125
ILLINOIS BELL TELEPHONE BUILDING
225 West Randolph
Holabird & Root, 1967

White marble polygonal piers, alternating with slender anodized aluminum mullions and vertical bands of dark glass, rise from the sidewalk to the summit.

C126
225 WEST WASHINGTON
Skidmore, Owings & Merrill, 1987

Adrian Smith, the S.O.M. partner-designer of this 28-story building, chose to relate the design to early Chicago School skyscrapers as well as to some more recent structures. His design is an interesting pastiche of Chicago elements: a base-shaft-top arrangement, Chicago windows, oriels at the corners, and an emphasis on broad vertical piers. One is struck, primarily, by the rich patterns of texture and color. The spandrels and piers are sheathed with precast concrete panels, which have been sandblasted to look like limestone and inset with panels of polished red granite. The recessed green window frames and glass complement the red color of the granite, while creating additional flat patterns. The base of the structure is of Napoleon red granite, with a tall entrance arch leading to the lobby of red veined marble with mahogany paneling. On the wall hangs an enlarged tapestry version of a detail of a stenciled pattern from Louis Sullivan's Stock Exchange trading room.

C127
ONE NORTH FRANKLIN
Skidmore, Owings & Merrill, 1992

Joseph Gonzalez, one of Skidmore's younger partners, designed this 38-story tower sheathed in pale gray granite, and topped by twin lighted towers reminiscent of the 30s. The red marble-clad base also has a deco appearance. Heavy black marble columns flank the entrance.

C128
303 WEST MADISON
Skidmore, Owings & Merrill, 1988

Joseph Gonzalez, assisted by Bruce Graham, designed this narrow 26-story tower, his first Chicago skyscraper. Gonzalez claims to have studied the work of Jenney, Root and Wright. Even though it has the base-shaft-summit arrangement and the Chicago windows, so characteristic of the Chicago School, the building has a complexity somewhat foreign to the Chicago tradition. It is interesting for its color combinations: flame-cut light gray and polished green granite, blue-green tinted glass, and dark red accents on the mullions. At the base, storefronts are entered directly from the sidewalk. At the center of the Franklin Street facade, the wall is indented giving focus to a set-back entrance. The lobby wall is truly remarkable, having an art-glass window 14 by 18 feet, influenced by Frank Lloyd Wright, but unique in its large circular pattern and its color scheme of shades of green and lavender. At the top of the building the mechanical floor is a flat-roofed loggia with skylights providing a play of light and shade.

C129
AT&T

100 South Franklin
Skidmore, Owings & Merrill, 1989

Adrian Smith is the S.O.M. designer responsible for this 60-story rectangular tube structure. A strong vertical emphasis created by the window groupings brings one's eye swiftly to the top where the design terminates in a climax of multiple finials. "Neo-moderne", deliberately retrograde, sometimes compared to Eliel Saarinen's 1922 Tribune Tower entry, the design displays a complexity undreamed of by the more restrained Saarinen. The facade, as well as the interiors, displays a dazzling array of materials, colors, and textures. Deep reddish-brown granite and lighter red granite on the base are highlighted with black granite, gold leaf and brass. Rose/beige granite with ornate silk-screened aluminum panels sheathes the tower above the fifth story.

C130
USG BUILDING

125 South Franklin
Skidmore, Owings & Merrill, 1989

Designed in tandem with the AT&T Building to the north, the two structures are joined with a five-story atrium.

C131
BROOKS BUILDING

223 West Jackson
Holabird & Roche, 1910

The Brooks Building, named for its developer, Peter C. Brooks of Boston, is one of the classic examples of the Chicago School because of the clarity with which its facades express the steel skeleton structure. Triple windows are recessed in each bay between strongly projecting piers with round moldings. The terra cotta facade shows some influence from Louis Sullivan's Gage building facade on Michigan Avenue. The piers in each building burst forth in ornament at the cornice level. The Brooks building is unusual in its use of green terra cotta for a frieze at the summit and green medallions contrasting with the ivory terra cotta used elsewhere.

BROOKS BUILDING

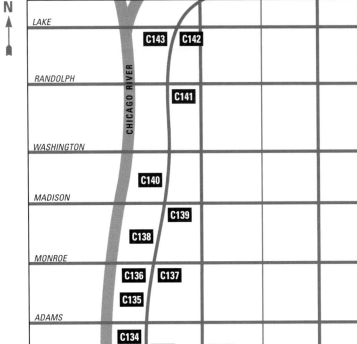

C132
311 SOUTH WACKER DRIVE

C133
SEARS TOWER
233 South Wacker Drive

C134
200 SOUTH WACKER DRIVE

C135
HARTFORD INSURANCE
BUILDING #2
150 South Wacker Drive

C136
HARTFORD INSURANCE
BUILDING
100 South Wacker Drive

C137
101 SOUTH WACKER DRIVE

C138
CHICAGO MERCANTILE
EXCHANGE
10 and 30 South Wacker Drive

C139
ONE SOUTH WACKER DRIVE

C140
CIVIC OPERA BUILDING
20 North Wacker Drive

C141
123 NORTH WACKER DRIVE

C142
333 WEST LAKE BUILDING

C143
GREAT LAKES BUILDING
180 North Wacker Drive

WACKER DRIVE

Once called Market Street, this corridor was lined with vegetable and meat markets and wholesale businesses. South of Washington Street was the "garment district," where some of the largest wholesale warehouses in the city were located. In the 1920s, the two-level Wacker Drive was created, named after Charles H. Wacker, president of the Chicago Planning Commission at the time. The character of the street has been transformed dramatically in the last twenty-five years with the construction of numerous office towers.

Along the South Branch of the Chicago River
from Van Buren to Lake Street

C132
311 SOUTH WACKER DRIVE
Kohn Pedersen Fox, 1990

This octagonal tower, designed by William Pedersen, is 65 stories and 970 feet high—the tallest reinforced concrete structure in the world. The extremely high-strength concrete has an additive, microsilica, a product of computer chips, only available since the 1970s. The whole is sheathed in patterns of pink and red Texas granite. Two flanking wings of the tower terminate at the fiftieth floor, while the octagon continues upward and finally terminates with a controversial, over-scaled, 70-foot, translucent cylinder with crenelations around its upper edges and four smaller, similar cylinders. At night the cylinders are ablaze with light given off by 2000 flourescent bulbs within. The focal point of the site is an 86-foot, barrel-vaulted wintergarden, which curiously combines forms of nineteenth century English market halls with Art Deco details. The interior is a beautiful space accented with a double row of embalmed palm trees and the somewhat baroque, bronze sculpture, *Gem of the Lake*, by sculptor Raymond Kaskey.

311 SOUTH WACKER DRIVE

C133
SEARS TOWER
233 South Wacker Drive
Skidmore, Owings & Merrill, 1974

The Sears Tower, built for the largest department store chain in the world, was for two decades the tallest building in the world at 1,454 feet and 110 stories. S.O.M. structural engineer Fazler Khan and architect Bruce Graham devised a highly rigid and extraordinarily economical system of construction, which they called the "bundled tube". The structure is that of nine rigid interlocking steel tubes, joined together. Each tube is a square, 75 feet on a side, framed in welded steel with columns on 15-foot centers. The larger plan, or the bundle of tubes, measures 225 feet on a side. Two tubes terminate at the fiftieth floor, two more stop at the 66th story, and two more at the 90th floor. Diagonal-member trusses bind the structure together (like rubber bands) at three different levels. This new system of construction made it possible to reduce the required amount of steel to thirty-three pounds per square foot, rather than the usual fifty or sixty. The $150 million structure took three years to build. A black anodized aluminum curtain wall sheathes the building. In 1985, Skidmore, Owings & Merrill added a four-story, glazed, barrel-vaulted atrium entrance on Wacker, somewhat incongruous with the design of the rest of the building. The tower with its entrance sits on a three-acre site paved in reddish-pink granite.

SEARS TOWER

C134
200 SOUTH WACKER DRIVE
Harry Weese & Associates, 1981

This unusual 38-story concrete-frame structure, sheathed with horizontal bands of white aluminum alternating with ribbons of glass, calls one's attention to itself by its unusual geometry. Squeezed onto a small, irregular site on the bank of the river, the tower has a slightly irregular, four-sided polygonal plan consistent from the ground through the thirty-first floor. The top seven stories rise shaft-like over the northeast portion of the building, creating a visual illusion that the entire structure is split into two triangle, joined by their hypotenuses. The 3-story lobby design is also a play on triangular form. Set back with diagonally sloping walls, it provides a wide, pleasant colonnade at the pedestrian level. Weese also designed a tiny riverfront park in 1988, which developer John Buck presented as a gift to the city.

HARTFORD INSURANCE BUILDING

200 SOUTH WACKER DRIVE

C135
HARTFORD INSURANCE BUILDING #2
150 South Wacker Drive
Skidmore, Owings & Merrill, 1971

Ten years later, S.O.M. built a 33-story building for Hartford Insurance, just to the south of their first structure, connected on ground level by a plaza and underground by a lower concourse. Like the earlier structure, it is a concrete skeleton, but with heavier piers to carry the greater weight. A strong visual contrast to the first, it is clad with polished granite, and its windows are set in the plane of the peripheral piers.

C136
HARTFORD INSURANCE BUILDING
100 South Wacker Drive
Skidmore, Owings & Merrill, 1959-61

Bruce Graham designed this 20-story structure as a reinforced concrete skeleton, whose slender columns on 21-foot centers, become progressively thinner as they rise. The grid-like skeleton is prominent on the exterior because the curtain walls are set well behind the peripheral, granite-clad columns. Ledges at each floor level provide shade for the offices and easy access to window walls for maintenance.

 101 SOUTH WACKER DRIVE

 CHICAGO MERCANTILE EXCHANGE

 ONE SOUTH WACKER DRIVE

C137
101 SOUTH WACKER DRIVE
Perkins & Will Partnership, 1963

A striking corporate image, built for U.S. Gypsum, was created by rotating the19-story steel-framed tower 45 degrees to the street, thereby visually separating the building from its neighbors. The plan is a square with its corners cut back, allowing for eight corner offices per story. The polyhedral shapes of the penthouse were inspired by the crystal of calcium sulfate, or gypsum. Faceted columns, sheathed in Vermont white marble, sit outside the wall plane and terminate in spiked finials. Contrasting with the columns in color and texture are recessed spandrels of rough-faced black slate and windows of dark gray glass.

C138
CHICAGO MERCANTILE EXCHANGE
10 and 30 South Wacker Drive
Fujikawa, Johnson & Associates,1883, 1988

This immense structure includes two 40-story towers, sheathed in red carnelian granite and gray solar glass, springing from a 12-story low-rise base. Designed by Fujikawa, who was trained under Mies van der Rohe, its spaces are highly functional. There are two gigantic, column-free trading rooms, each covered with plush acoustical material several feet thick. Here options and futures are sold on commodities. The main trading floor, 40,000 square feet in area, contains 21 octagonal trading pits and is spanned by six huge 80-ton steel trusses. The second trading room, above the other, is almost as large with 35,000 square feet. The architects devised an unusual method of diverting the weight of the towers around the trading rooms. Each tower floor projects 1/8 inch beyond the one below it, up to the twenty-first story, where it reaches a cantilever of 32 feet. In the stories above, the process is reversed. The towers have "serrated" corners, allowing for as many as sixteen corner offices per floor.

C139
ONE SOUTH WACKER DRIVE
Murphy/Jahn, 1983

This 40-story, silvery glass box designed by Helmut Jahn attracts the public through its glitz and bold geometric, angled setbacks. Multistory atriums are set above and below each setback, while a tiara-shaped penthouse on the top houses mechanical equipment. While visually stimulating, certain disturbing qualities are ever-present: the lack of scale, the black shapes against the silver creating huge negative-positive illusions, the zig-zag shapes at the sidewalk level which recall corbel arches, here hanging in space rather than supporting the structure as they traditionally would.

CIVIC OPERA BUILDING

C140
CIVIC OPERA BUILDING
20 North Wacker Drive
Graham, Anderson, Probst & White, 1928-29

Samuel Insull conceived and funded this $23 million project on the eve of the great depression. The grand opening featured *Aida* just six days after the great stock market crash. The structure, which contributed to the bankruptcy of the Adler & Sullivan Auditorium, ultimately led also to Insull's bankruptcy. Because of the shape of the structure, it is jokingly dubbed "Insull's Throne." The 45-story office tower wraps the west side of the opera house, while 22-story wings frame it on the north and south. The style, interior and exterior, is French Renaissance with Art Deco overtones. The facades are of limestone with terra cotta trim and cast iron window spandrels. A 35-foot high colonnade of rectangular columns with chamfered corners and unique capitals provides shelter for pedestrians. Ornate entrances at either end lead to the opera house auditorium and the theater. A center entrance leads to the office tower. Jules Guerin was in charge of the beautiful interior decoration, a color scheme of red, salmon and gold. Stunning patterns and murals adorn the ceilings and walls.

C141
123 NORTH WACKER DRIVE
Perkins & Will Partnership, 1986

Ralph Johnson, vice-president of Perkins & Will, designed this 30-story tower with a facade of red and gray polished and flamed-finished granite. In part he borrowed design elements from the Civic Opera and other neighboring buildings: the pyramidal roof, the 24-foot oculus, and the 30-foot high pedestrian arcade. Blocky shapes at the corners of the structure contrast with the glazed walls in between. The pyramidal structure at the summit is for mechanical equipment; it is actually composed of horizontal pipes through which light passes at night. On the ground floor, the two-story shallow lobby is of white, gray and pink marble with a fountain, which runs down the center wall.

C142
333 WEST LAKE BUILDING
D.H. Burnham & Company, 1898

Originally the Franklin MacVeagh Co., this nine-story brick structure is well-proportioned and clearly exhibits its structural pier and beam system of construction. The building stands on the site of one of Chicago's first buildings, the Eagle Exchange Tavern, later replaced by the so-called Wigwam, where Abraham Lincoln was nominated for President.

C143
GREAT LAKES BUILDING
180 North Wacker Drive
Holabird & Roche, 1912

This beautiful red brick structure has strongly projecting piers, which rise the full 6-story height. The top of the walls project outward with corbeled courses of brick, providing a simple and elegant visual closure to the design. The building was tastefully renovated in 1981.

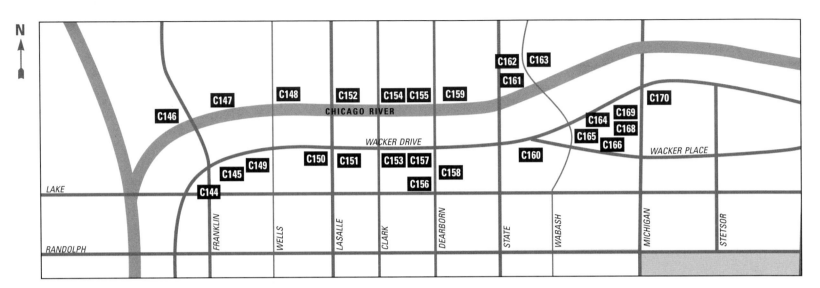

C144
NUVEEN BUILDING
333 West Wacker

C145
225 WEST WACKER DRIVE

C146
APPAREL CENTER
350 North Orleans

C147
MERCHANDISE MART
350 North Wells

C148
HELENE CURTIS BUILDING
325 North Wells

C149
ENGINEERING BUILDING
205 West Wacker Drive

C150
BUILDERS BUILDING
222 North LaSalle

C151
LASALLE - WACKER
BUILDING
221 North LaSalle

C152
REID, MURDOCH BUILDING
320 North Clark

C153
R.R. DONNELLEY BUILDING
77 West Wacker Drive

C154
QUAKER TOWER
321 North Clark

C155
WESTIN HOTEL
320 North Dearborn

C156
200 NORTH DEARBORN

C157
55 WEST WACKER DRIVE

C158
LEO BURNETT BUILDING
35 West Wacker Drive

C159
MARINA CITY
300 North State

C160
JEWELERS BUILDING
35 East Wacker Drive

C161
IBM BUILDING
330 North Wabash

C162
IBM PARKING FACILITY
401 North State

C163
CHICAGO SUN-TIMES
BUILDING
401 North Wabash

C164
MATHER TOWER
75 East Wacker Drive

C165
SEVENTEENTH CHURCH OF
CHRIST SCIENTIST
55 East Wacker Drive

C166
WACKER TOWER
68 East Wacker Place

C167
CARBIDE & CARBON BUILD-
ING
230 North Michigan

C168
320 NORTH MICHIGAN

C169
360 NORTH MICHIGAN

C170
333 NORTH MICHIGAN

CHICAGO RIVER

Main Branch from North Wacker

to North Michigan

The Chicago River's main branch was originally the heart of the city. Along its south bank was South Water Street, and in the 1830s, log cabins, Chicago's original structures, were clustered here. Before bridges were built, ferries plowed back and forth. During much of the last century, shipping interests, meat-packing warehouses and grain elevators pressed the river's edge, causing many other businesses to turn their backs to it. Because the waters were polluted, the city decided in the 1890s to reverse the flow of the river, which they did. Another daring city planning decision came in the 1920s, when the Chicago Plan Commission decided to build a double-decked belt road, now Wacker Drive, named after Charles Wacker, the first chairman of the plan commission. Many of the bridge-houses also date from this era.

203 NORTH LASALLE

MERCHANDISE MART

C144
NUVEEN BUILDING

33 West Wacker Drive
Kohn Pedersen Fox, 1983

The riverfront facade of the Nuveen Building bends its 365-foot elliptical facade, mirroring the gentle curve of the Chicago River. The 36-story structure, which sits on a triangular site, presents a prismatic facade toward the corner of Lake and Franklin Streets. Many features are borrowed from Art Deco, such as the sleek materials: green Vermont marble and gray granite, columns of black polished granite and veined green marble, hardware and railings of brushed stainless steel. Accenting the base are 26 exaggerated, louvered vent covers. The upper floors are sheathed with horizontal bands of two shades of green-tinted reflective glass.

C145
225 WEST WACKER DRIVE

Kohn Pedersen Fox, 1989

Sheathed in a skin of Spanish gray and impala black granite, 225 West Wacker is designed to be traditional, yet modern. The 31-story structure relates to its neighbor, the Nuveen Building, in such ways as its semi-circular green marble rotunda, its arcade, and its medallion grills. In addition, it has picked up other Art Deco elements from nearby buildings of the 1920s. The four exaggerated aluminum lanterns at the summit of 225 have spiral casings, bobbin-like spires, and metal bridges between them, a trite a reference to Chicago bridges.

C146
APPAREL CENTER

350 North Orleans Street
Skidmore, Owings & Merrill, 1976

The lower part of this 23-story building is nearly windowless, partly to save energy and partly because natural light was not desirable for the showrooms. The absence of windows and the uniformity of the pre-cast concrete sheathing make the structure somewhat monotonous. The top of the structure, however, is a Holiday Inn model, with windows, and with a central nine-story atrium.

C147
MERCHANDISE MART

350 North Wells
Graham, Anderson, Probst & White, 1928-31

This wholesale exhibition building, covering two city blocks, was commissioned by Marshall Field & Company to replace their previous warehouse built by H.H. Richardson. An 18-story structure with a 7-story tower, the Merchandise Mart has 97 acres of floor space. Until the Sears Tower was built, it was the largest commercial structure in the world. In 1945 Joseph P. Kennedy purchased the building for back taxes, and it remained in Kennedy possession until recently.

The Mart is a good example of Art Deco, with a central tower over the entrance, four corner projecting bays, octagonal hipped copper roofs, windows in vertical bands and continuous mullions sheathed in buff Bedford limestone. Much of the original Art Deco ornament has been preserved in the lobby, including lighting fixtures, mailboxes, door hardware, and elevator doors. The lobby also includes a marvelous series of fifteen Jules Guerin murals depicting markets around the world. The building has recently been restored, and a two-story mall has been added on the first two floors with new entrances at the corners.

C148
HELENE CURTIS BUILDING

325 North Wells

L.G. Hallberg, 1914; Renovation, Booth/Hansen & Associates, 1985

Formerly known as the Exhibitors Building, this ten-story Chicago School structure was built for light industrial and display functions. Lawrence Booth transformed the warehouse into a more sophisticated, eye-catching structure with an elegant interior. His manipulation of space, especially of the top one-and-a-half story addition, is arbitrary and somewhat shocking, although Booth claimed that the new spaces were determined directly by the needs of the company. The rounded glass penthouse serves as the corporate board room. Green glass was utilized throughout, because it complemented the old red brick and also blended with the color of the Chicago River.

C149
ENGINEERING BUILDING

205 West Wacker Drive

The Burnham Brothers, 1928; Renovation, Himmel Bonner Architects, 1982

This 23-story, Art Deco skyscraper was designed by two sons of Daniel H. Burnham: Hubert and Daniel H., Jr. Stylized ornament adorns the facades at the third story, all stories above the nineteenth, and on projections at the roofline.

C150
BUILDERS BUILDING

222 North LaSalle Street

Graham, Anderson, Probst and White, 1927; Addition and Renovation, Skidmore, Owings & Merrill, 1986

Originally planned with exhibition spaces for the building industry arranged around a marvelously ornate four-story galleried rotunda, the Builders Building has been restored under the direction of Adrian Smith. His west addition is a beautifully sensitive example of con-texturalism. While maintaining the character of the older building, a new modern structure was added in complete harmony with the original. Contrasting with the limestone cladding of the 1927 building, the new building is sheathed in granite with dark glazed oriels. The colonnaded upper stories of the old building are matched by simplified columns in the new section. Capping the whole, above the cornice, Smith added a four-story penthouse in the form of a mansard roof.

C151
LASALLE-WACKER BUILDING

221 North LaSalle

Holabird & Root with Rebori, Wentworth, Dewey & McCormick, 1930

The designer of the 41-story LaSalle-Wacker Building was apparently Andrew Rebori, judging by drawings at the Chicago Historical Society, although he collaborated with Holabird and Root. The plan, massing and window groupings are quite suggestive of other Holabird and Root buildings of the depression era. The lobby retains its Art Deco character.

C152
REID, MURDOCH BUILDING

320 North Clark
George Nimmons, 1913

This former warehouse of the Reid, Murdoch Company is now the City of Chicago Central Office building. Built of reinforced concrete, the eight-story building emphasizes its structure, typical of the Chicago School. Nimmons, who had much experience designing warehouses, chose a warm, dark red brick facing and enlivened it with brown terra cotta insets. A handsome square clock in the center of the structure rises three stories above the roof and provides a visual focus.

BUILDERS BUILDING

R.R. DONNELLEY BUILDING

QUAKER TOWER

WESTIN HOTEL

C153
R.R. DONNELLEY BUILDING
77 West Wacker Drive
Ricardo Bofill Arquitectura, with DeStefano/Goettsch, 1992

Chicago's only building by Spanish architect Ricardo Bofill, this 50-story glass office skyscraper is a stripped-down classical structure of Cyclopian proportions. Clad with attenuated classical pilasters, entablatures and pediments in flame-cut white granite, the forms contrast with wide expanses of silver reflective glass. Seen from a distance the building provides no clues to its size and it appears more like a hollow skeleton than a solid form. Bofill's classicism, complexity and de-emphasis on structural form provide a contrast to the rational architecture for which this city is known. Although the stacked, multi-story temple forms may be disturbing to traditionalists, the building has a unique beauty.

C154
QUAKER TOWER
32l North Clark
Skidmore, Owings & Merrill,1987

The 35-story Quaker Tower and the much smaller Westin Hotel to its east were called by Paul Gapp of the *Chicago Tribune* the "Odd Couple." The owners of Quaker Oats preferred a conservative, rectangular cube design with a flat roof, so Bruce Graham of Skidmore agreed to "do a beautiful box...to show how glass skin could really be done." A structural steel skeleton is hung with curtain walls of tinted green glass, blue glass spandrels, and curved stainless steel mullions. The riverbank between Clark and Dearborn is developed as a pedestrian Riverfront Park with concrete terraces and plantings.

C155
WESTIN HOTEL
320 North Dearborn
Hellmuth, Obata & Kassabaum, 1987

Developed by Japan Air Lines and Tishman Realty as the Nikko Hotel, and designed by a St. Louis architectural firm, this 20-story structure is sleek, modern, and expensive, with a "contemporary Japanese" look. Obata achieved a distinct identity for the building by giving the roof-line an unusual profile, which he repeated on the entry pavilion to the north and on the low pavilion which connects the structure to Quaker Tower on the west. Banks of dark gray glazed bay windows alternate with vertical bands of polished light gray granite. Looking out across the river, hotel guests can view a small Japanese-style Riverfront Park, designed by Japanese architect Kenzo Tange.

C156
200 NORTH DEARBORN
Lisec & Biederman, Ltd., 1989

Just south of the Lakeside Bank Building is this 47-story, 309-unit apartment building, built of exposed, reinforced concrete. The base unit extends to Clark Street and includes a concourse with shopping and terraced gardens. The east and west facades terminate with double gables.

C157
55 WEST WACKER DRIVE
C.F. Murphy Associates, 1968

Originally built for Blue Cross-Blue Shield, this 15-story building boldly expresses its structure. Its massive paired piers are a beige concrete, textured with vertical grooves, while its recessed spandrels of the same color contrast by their smoothness.

C158
LEO BURNETT BUILDING
35 West Wacker Drive
Kevin Roche-John Dinkeloo & Associates, 1989

Built as the world headquarters for the Leo Burnett advertising firm, this 50-story tower attracts attention for its bold shape and strong surface patterns. It has been compared to a "hounds-tooth suit" for the repetitive rhythms of dark and light. Walls of gray and green granite are punched with deeply-set windows, each bisected by a half-round stainless steel and black mullion. The scale is immense, with a five-story colonnade at the base, repeated at the 15th-story setback and again at the summit. The monumental lobby has beautifully designed Deco-revival features.

C159
MARINA CITY
300 North State
Bertrand Goldberg, 1964, 1967

Goldberg's unique and dramatic, corncob-shaped towers have become a visual symbol for Chicago. When built, the 62-story, 588-foot-high structures were the tallest apartment buildings and the tallest reinforced concrete structures in the world. The complex includes an 80-boat marina, shops, bowling alley, pool, ice-skating rink and restaurants. In addition there is a ten-story office building and a saddle-shaped building with a hyperbolic paraboloid shell, originally a theater. The construction of the towers was unusual for the time: each has a 30-foot diameter, cylindrical core, from which sixty circular floor slabs cantilever out, partially supported by two rings of peripheral concrete columns. The first 17 floors are helical parking garages. The nine hundred apartments in the two towers are pie-shaped with semi-circular cantilevered balconies, which give the building a scalloped, or petal-like, appearance.

C160
JEWELERS BUILDING
35 East Wacker Drive
Thielbar & Fugard, with Giaver & Dinkleberg, 1924-26

One of the most lavishly Baroque office buildings in Chicago, this wedding-cake-like structure seems appropriate for clients who were jewelers. The letters "JB" are worked extensively into the elaborate cream-colored terra cotta cladding. The name was changed to the Pure Oil Building in 1926 and later to the North American Life Insurance Building. Today it is known by its address.

The 24-story main block of the structure is surmounted at each corner by small neo-classical temple-like structures, actually water tanks supported by columns. A recent remodeling turned the two-story bases of these forms into conference rooms. The twenty-fourth story at one time had also a roof promenade. A smaller, 17-story tower rises from this level and is crowned by a domed penthouse, now the office of Helmut Jahn. Originally the core of the main block was its parking garage. Tenants could drive from Lower Wacker into the building, and without leaving their car, could be taken by elevator to their office floor, where they would park in proximity to their office.

IBM BUILDING

C161
IBM BUILDING
330 North Wabash
Ludwig Mies van der Rohe, 1967-71

The ultimate in refined proportions and minimalist form, this 52-story glass tower embodies Mies's principle, "Less is more." It was the last building Mies designed before his death in 1969 and was completed in 1972 under the direction of Bruce Conterato in Mies's office. The structure is of materials which Mies had long favored, a steel frame with a curtain wall of anodized aluminum and bronze-tinted glass. As always, details are all carefully studied. In the building's high, set-back glass lobby, the walls are paneled with travertine. A small bust of Mies by sculptor Marino Marini is displayed.

C162
IBM PARKING FACILITY
401 North State
George Schipporeit, Inc., 1974

This 12-story garage for 800 cars was designed by a former student and employee of Mies. Its curvilinear screen walls of vertical fins of Cor-ten steel provide an interesting contrast to the IBM office building, which it serves.

C163
CHICAGO SUN-TIMES BUILDING
401 North Wabash
Naess & Murphy, 1955-57

The aluminum-clad, 7-story *Sun-Times* Building seems even shorter than its seven stories because of the contrast it makes with the skyscrapers around it. It has a somewhat floating appearance, because its ground story is recessed. Its top floor, which houses executive offices, is also set back, protected by a projecting slab roof.

C164
MATHER TOWER
75 East Wacker Drive
Herbert H. Riddle, 1928

This vertical, Gothic revival tower, clad in white terra cotta, was the tallest in Chicago when built. Extremely tall for its 65-by-100 foot site, its main block rises 24 stories with small set-backs, then is surmounted by an 18-story, octagonal tower, which reportedly has the smallest floor space per story of any building in the Loop. Originally called Mather Tower after its owner Alonzo Mather, it later was named the Lincoln Tower, and today is known by its address.

C165
SEVENTEENTH CHURCH OF CHRIST SCIENTIST
55 East Wacker Drive
Harry Weese & Associates, 1968

This unusual, semi-circular structure, faced in travertine marble, was designed to fit a small, irregular site. Its recessed glass lobby provides access to Sunday School rooms below and an auditorium above. Adjoining to the east is a triangular, seven-story office wing.

SEVENTEENTH CHURCH OF CHRIST SCIENTIST

C166
WACKER TOWER
(Chicago Motor Club Building)
68 East Wacker Place
Holabird & Root, 1928; John Vinci, Adaptive reuse, 1997

This slender, 15-story, limestone-faced building, formerly the headquarters of the Chicago Motor Club, is classical in its formal, symmetrical arrangement. Both architects had studied at the Ecole des Beaux-Arts in Paris, where Art Deco originated and was all the rage. The beautiful, lofty, Art Deco lobby displaying an impressive large mural by John Warner Norton has been retained. John Vinci is currently converting the building to fourteen condominiums.

C167
CARBIDE & CARBON BUILDING
230 North Michigan
Burnham Brothers, 1929

Two of Daniel Burnham's sons, Hubert and Daniel, Jr., who had worked for their father and continued in business as partners after his death, designed this dramatic 40-story, set-back tower. Perhaps the building's dark color was chosen because of its similarity to the color or coal or carbon. The three-story base of the building is of black polished granite with black marble and bronze trim. The upper facade walls are of dark green terra cotta with gold metal trim and near the very top an extensive amount of actual gold leaf. The lobby with its brass and embossed glass ornament is a masterpiece of Art Deco.

C168
320 NORTH MICHIGAN
Booth/Hansen & Associates, 1983

The facade of this narrow 26-story concrete grid structure is enlivened with articulated projecting moldings. The ground floor, entered through stripped-down classical columns, is commercial. Floors 2 through 13 are for offices and above are condominiums. On top, between three stepped-back stories, is an extravagant gabled penthouse with greenhouse. Throughout the building, windows face only east and west, while rose-colored infill panels form a pattern on the exposed north and south faces.

C169
360 NORTH MICHIGAN AVENUE
Alfred S. Alschuler, 1923

This eclectic neo-classical office building was originally the London Guarantee Building and later the Stone Container Building. It is noted for its Roman temple style cupola on top.

C170
333 NORTH MICHIGAN AVENUE
Holabird & Root, 1928

One of Chicago's most important buildings in the fashionable Art Deco style, the inspiration for this slender tower came from Eliel Saarinen's design for the Tribune Tower as well as the avant-garde French designs of the time. The stylized and geometric decor of the Parisian *Exposition des Arts Decoratifs* of 1925 was beginning to attract admirers in America. Above the building's polished marble base, which is accented by round flush windows, its gray limestone facade makes a strong vertical statement through the grouping of the windows and their continuous mullions. The north part of the structure is 35 stories, while the main block to the south is 24 stories. Because this building stands on the site of Fort Dearborn, seven-foot high incised reliefs by Fred M. Torrey decorate the fifth story facade with depictions of early Chicago pioneers, while inside, on the elevator doors, are sculpted reliefs by Edgar Miller.

CARBIDE & CARBON BUILDING

333 NORTH MICHIGAN AVENUE

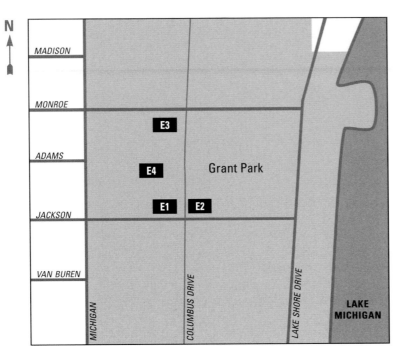

N

MADISON

MONROE

E3

ADAMS

E4

Grant Park

E1 E2

JACKSON

VAN BUREN

MICHIGAN

COLUMBUS DRIVE

LAKE SHORE DRIVE

LAKE MICHIGAN

E1
SCHOOL OF THE ART INSTITUTE
Columbus Drive and Jackson

E2
PETRILLO MUSIC SHELL
Columbus Drive and Jackson

E3
STOCK EXCHANGE ARCH
Columbus Drive and Monroe

E4
GOODMAN THEATER
200 South Columbus Drive

GRANT PARK

In a subdivision map of 1836, the land east of Michigan Avenue was designated as "public ground, forever to remain vacant of building." The City of Chicago, however, in 1872, commissioned W.W. Boyington to design and construct an iron and glass structure, the Inter-State Industrial Exposition Building east of Michigan between Adams and Jackson. The building was demolished for the 1892 construction of the present Art Institute. Montgomery Ward, who owned two buildings facing the park on Michigan Avenue, sued the city four times for infringing on public rights. Grant Park, as we know it today, is also partly the result of Daniel Burnham's Chicago Plan of 1909, commissioned by a group of Chicago businessmen. The Chicago Plan called for symmetrical geometric landscaping, yacht basins, pleasure piers and athletic grounds. Burnham was able to watch the reconstruction of Grant Park from his office in the Railway Exchange Building.

EAST

STOCK EXCHANGE ARCH

E1
SCHOOL OF THE ART INSTITUTE
Columbus and Jackson
Skidmore, Owings & Merrill, 1977

Walter Netsch , the Skidmore partner responsible for this design, had previously constructed the Architecture and Art Building, along with other buildings of complex geometry at the University of Illinois. Following many dialogues with the faculty of the school of the Art Institute, Netsch's design here is somewhat more restrained and functional, although at the same time he retains many angular projections and recesses.

E2
PETRILLO MUSIC SHELL
Columbus Drive at Jackson
Chicago Park District, 1878

The shell, where free concerts are performed all summer, was designed as a demountable structure in order to avoid the ban on the construction of new structures in Grant Park.

E3
STOCK EXCHANGE ARCH
Columbus Drive at Monroe
Adler & Sullivan, 1993

This magnificent arch was the entry to the Chicago Stock Exchange at 30 North LaSalle Street until the demise of the building in 1972. The reconstruction of the Trading Room of the exchange was subsequently installed in the Art Institute, near the Columbus Drive entrance. The rich decoration of this room, related to the ornament of the arch outside, is not to be missed.

E4
GOODMAN THEATER
200 South Columbus Drive
Howard Van Doren Shaw, 1926

Also part of the Art Institute is this small theater, which has an elegant neo-classical facade. Its 683 seats are arranged to provide comfortable space and excellent viewing for performances.

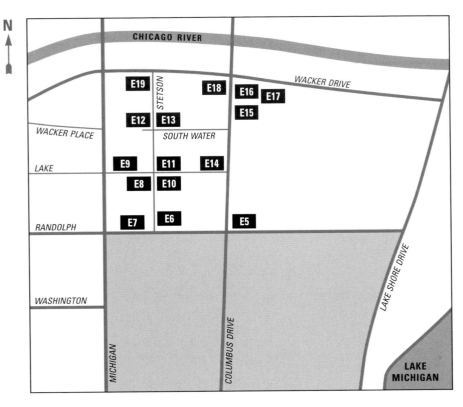

E5
BLUE CROSS-BLUE SHIELD BUILDING
300 East Randolph

E6
AMOCO BUILDING
200 East Randolph

E7
ONE PRUDENTIAL PLAZA
130 East Randolph

E8
TWO PRUDENTIAL PLAZA
180 North Stetson

E9
BOULEVARD TOWERS
205-225 North Michigan

E10
AMOCO PLAZA PORTALS
200 North Columbus Drive

E11
ATHLETIC CLUB ILLINOIS
211 North Stetson

E12
TWO ILLINOIS CENTER
233 North Michigan

E13
HYATT REGENCY CHICAGO
151 East Wacker Drive

E14
FAIRMONT HOTEL
200 North Columbus Drive

E15
FIRE STATION CF-21
259 North Columbus Drive

E16
THREE ILLINOIS CENTER
303 East Wacker Drive

E17
SWISSOTEL
323 East Wacker Drive

E18
COLUMBUS PLAZA
233 East Wacker Drive

E19
ONE ILLINOIS CENTER
111 East Wacker Drive

ILLINOIS CENTER

Illinois Center is an 83-acre site between Grant Park, Lake Michigan, Michigan Avenue and the Chicago River. Most of the buildings in the area were built since 1875 on railway air rights. The district is multi-functional with hotels, office structures and apartment buildings. Since none of the buildings are older than the Prudential, built in 1955, the area has a very modern character, lacking in the variety that one finds just north and west of the area. The influence of Mies van der Rohe is everywhere.

From Columbus Drive and Randolph to Michigan, to Lake, to Stetson, to South Water, to Columbus Drive, to East Wacker Drive

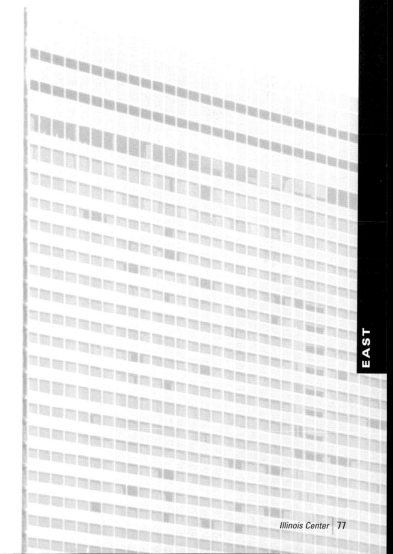

EAST

BLUE CROSS-BLUE SHIELD BUILDING

AMOCO BUILDING

E5
BLUE CROSS-BLUE SHIELD BUILDING
300 East Randolph
Lohan Associates, 1996

After a several-year lull in Loop high rise construction because of the overbuilding spree of the 1980s, Blue Cross Blue Shield built this massive 30-story building on a beautiful site facing Grant Park. The insurance company's concern was to build enough space for their present needs, but to have the possibility of expanding upward in the future. Dirk Lohan designed the structure with steel columns which extend a foot above the roof line and with foundations adequate to accommodate 24 additional stories. An atrium sandwiched between two concrete utility cores along the north wall brings light within. The structure is enclosed by a subdued steel and glass curtain wall.

E6
AMOCO BUILDING
200 East Randolph
Edward Durell Stone, 1974

At 80-stories and a height of 1136 feet, the Amoco Building was for a brief time the tallest structure in the world, barely surpassing the John Hancock Building, although later in the same year, the Sears Tower took the honor, making the Amoco the second tallest building in Chicago. Its verticality and absence of visible horizontal members removes any sense of scale. The windows are arranged as vertical bands of glass wedged between V-shaped columns, which conceal piping. The building's original cladding of Carrara marble was sliced too thin for Chicago's extreme temperature changes, causing the slabs to warp, crack and fall off. It was decided to remove the marble and reclad with thicker granite panels, a job which cost the company approximately $80 million and resulted in suits against the architects and contractors.

E7
ONE PRUDENTIAL PLAZA

130 East Randolph
Naess & Murphy, 1955

The first major skyscraper built in Chicago after World War II and the first building built on Illinois Central air rights, the Prudential Building, as it was originally called, is a 41-story steel skeleton with an aluminum and limestone curtain wall. Embedded in the wall is Alfonso Iannelli's 65-ton relief sculpture of the firm's trademark, the *Rock of Gibraltar.* It was briefly the world's fifth tallest building, and remained Chicago's tallest structure for a decade.

E8
TWO PRUDENTIAL PLAZA

180 North Stetson
Loebl, Schlossman & Hackl, 1988

Donald Hackl designed this 64-story, multifaceted, pyramidal-topped tower with cascading chevron shapes. Contrasting with the 1955 Prudential building in its height and shape, it is structurally united with the earlier building through the two five-story atrium lobbies and the plaza design. In addition, the facades are visually unified by similar verticality and related shades of gray stone, although granite is used here instead of limestone as in the first tower.

E9
BOULEVARD TOWERS

205-225 North Michigan
Fujikawa, Johnson & Associates, 1981, 1985

Continuing the aesthetic of Illinois One, Two and Three, Boulevard Towers has a central 19-story unit joining a 24-story tower on the north and a 44-story tower on the south.

E10
AMOCO PLAZA PORTALS

200 North Columbus Drive
Perkins & Will, 1986

To provide the Amoco Building ground-level visibility and to offer pedestrians an attractive entrance, Wojciech Madeyski of Perkins & Will designed identical portals of granite, marble and bronze at the east end of Lake Street and at Columbus Drive. Each triangular-topped portal invites the visitor to the Amoco building either through a formal plaza or by descending to a lower level underground walkway.

ONE AND TWO PRUDENTIAL PLAZA

ATHLETIC CLUB ILLINOIS

E11
ATHLETIC CLUB ILLINOIS
211 North Stetson
Kisho Kurokawa, 1989

This low building amidst towering skyscrapers is the first American design by Tokyo architect Kisho Kurokawa. A reinforced concrete modular frame with its structural system expressed on the perimeter in steel, it relates to the Miesian Chicago tradition as well as to Japanese modular buildings. The four vertical rooftop towers mirror the verticality of the highrises around it. The interior has a six-level atrium, mostly below grade, with a 110-foot high rock climbing wall.

E12
TWO ILLINOIS CENTER
233 North Michigan
Fujikawa, Conterato, Lohan & Associates, 1973

Built after Mies's death by Mies's successor firm, this office building is a twin to the earlier One Illinois Center.

E13
HYATT REGENCY CHICAGO
151 East Wacker Drive

A. Epstein & Sons, 1974, 1980

The largest hotel in the Hyatt chain includes two 33-story towers at right angles and a four-story glass wintergarden. The brick facing of the structures is a contrast to the buildings around it.

E14
FAIRMONT HOTEL
200 North Columbus Drive
Hellmuth, Obata, & Kassabaum, 1988

Stylistically more traditional and ornamental than most of its neighbors, the 37-story Fairmont Hotel is an L-shaped structure with chamfered corners, shallow bays, and a pleasing pale rose granite sheathing. An octagonal turret with a flagpole accents the peaked, green copper roof. The hotel lobby is octagonal with a sunken seating area in its center.

E15
FIRE STATION CF-21
259 North Columbus Drive
Fujikawa, Johnson & Associates, 1981

At the base of Three Illinois Center, this small station is a gem of the Miesian aesthetic.

E16
THREE ILLINOIS CENTER
303 East Wacker Drive
Fujikawa, Johnson & Associates, 1980

The clients who commissioned Illinois One and Two chose architects who worked in the Mies office on the design of the earlier buildings. The 28-story office building is almost identical to the earlier structures.

E17
SWISSOTEL
323 East Wacker Drive
Harry Weese & Associates, 1988

Alternate bands of silver and gray glass gently wrap the walls of this dramatic 43-story triangular reinforced concrete tower. The entrance is via a pavilion with a space-frame cover which, because of its triangular components, aesthetically complements the whole. The interiors by Merchant Associates of Los Angeles include a winding stainless steel staircase in the lobby, much cherry wood and brass, and a subdued color scheme.

E18
COLUMBUS PLAZA
233 East Wacker Drive
Fujikawa, Conterato, Lohan & Associates, 1980

Concrete was used for this apartment building, which blends with the dominant Miesian steel-and-glass aesthetic, which pervades Illinois Center.

E19
ONE ILLINOIS CENTER
111 East Wacker Drive
Mies van der Rohe, 1970

This 29-story structure has a reinforced concrete skeleton with large 30-foot square bays, concrete stiffening walls at the core, and coffered concrete floors. It is sheathed with curtain walls of bronze anodized aluminum and bronze-tinted glass. On the lower level are shops and restaurants, while the upper floors hold a million square feet of office space. The building occupies only half the lot.

SWISSOTEL

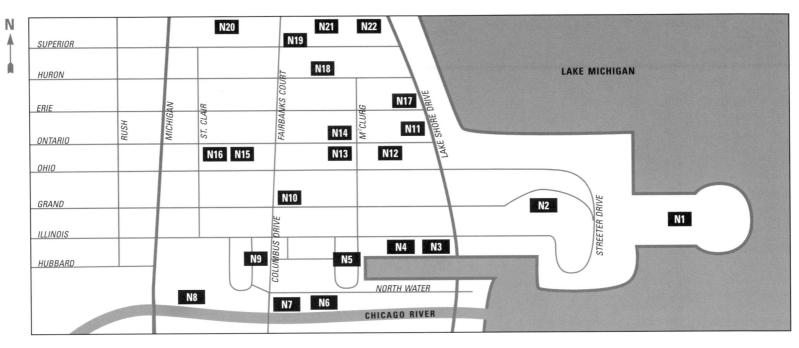

N1
NAVY PIER
600 East Grand

N2
LAKEPOINT TOWER
505 North Lake Shore Drive

N3
NORTH PIER APARTMENT
TOWER
474 North Lake Shore Drive

N4
NORTH PIER TERMINAL
435 East Illinois

N5
CITYFRONT PLACE
400-480 North McClurg Court
N6
CENTENNIAL FOUNTAIN
*McClurg Court Esplanade at
the River*

N7
SHERATON CHICAGO
301 East North Water

N8
GLEACHER CENTER
OF THE UNIVERSITY OF
CHICAGO
*450 North Cityfront Plaza
Drive*

N9
NBC TOWER
454 North Columbus Drive

N10
TIME-LIFE BUILDING
541 North Fairbanks Court

N11
ONTARIO CENTRE
446 East Ontario

N12
401 EAST ONTARIE

N13
MCCLURG COURT CENTER
333 East Ontario

N14
CBS BUILDING
630 North McClurg Court

N15
237 EAST ONTARIO

N-16
ARTS CLUB
211 East Ontario

N17
LAKE SHORE PLACE
680 North Lake Shore Drive

N18
PRENTICE WOMEN'S
HOSPITAL AND
MATERNITY CENTER
333 East Superior

N19
TARRY MEDICAL RESEARCH
AND EDUCATION BUILDING
300 East Superior

N20
AMERICAN DENTAL
ASSOCIATION BUILDING
211 East Chicago Avenue

N21
NORTHWESTERN
UNIVERSITY,
CHICAGO CAMPUS
303-357 East Chicago Avenue

N22
ARTHUR RUBLOFF BUILDING
750 North Lake Shore Drive

STREETERVILLE

Streeterville has traditionally been defined as the Near North district, bounded by the river, Chicago Avenue, the lake and St. Clair. It was named for the infamous sea captain, George Wellington Streeter, who lived on his shipwrecked boat near the present location of Navy Pier. When sand piled up around his vessel, he sold lots and proclaimed it as "The District of Lake Michigan." Streeter was constantly in court battles over his land, which he eventually lost. The portion of Streeterville south of Grand Avenue has assumed the name Cityfront Center. Since 1986, under the planning and supervision of Dirk Lohan, this area has experienced active development.

LAKEPOINT TOWER

N1
NAVY PIER
600 East Grand
Charles S. Frost, 1916; Benjamin Thompson, 1995

This 3000-foot long pier, once the world's largest, was until World War II an important passenger and freight terminal. From 1945 to 1965, it functioned as the Chicago campus of the University of Illinois. Today it is a complex conglomeration of various entertainment and convention structures and spaces.

N2
LAKEPOINT TOWER
505 North Lake Shore Drive
Schipporeit-Heinrich Associates; Graham, Anderson, Probst & White, associate architects; Alfred Caldwell, site plan, 1968

This dramatic, seventy-story tower on the lakefront was the tallest apartment building as well as the highest reinforced concrete building in the world when built. Its designers, George Schipporeit and John Heinrich, who had both studied with and worked for Mies van der Rohe, paid homage to their mentor in this curvilinear structure based on Mies's 1921 unbuilt design for an apartment tower in Berlin. Lake Point Tower is a structural masterpiece, supported primarily by a rigid triangular core, which absorbs wind forces and contains the elevators. The floor slabs are carried by the core as well as by reinforced concrete peripheral columns. Its bronze-colored glass curtain wall gives the building an ephemeral quality, especially when seen at sunrise or sunset, when the glass is ablaze with the colorful reflections of light.

N3
NORTH PIER APARTMENT TOWER
474 North Lake Shore Drive
Dubin, Dubin & Moutoussamy and Florian/Wierzbowski, 1990

This new 61-story tower has 505 apartment units in 48 stories above a 13-story parking garage. Its concrete frame supports a curtain wall of concrete panels cast with a sprinkle of granite chips. For visual interest, the architects gave five different colors to the panels.

N4
NORTH PIER TERMINAL
435 East Illinois (at Peshtigo Street)
Christian A. Eckstorm, 1905-1920; Adaptive Reuse: Booth/Hansen & Associates, 1986-88

Lawrence Booth is responsible for converting this formerly dilapidated warehouse structure into a lively entertainment center. He created stronger visual appeal by adding one-story penthouses with pyramidal roofs for freight elevator equipment. He drew attention to the entrances on the Illinois Street facade by constructing fan-shaped, steel, cable-suspended canopies. On the south facade, he opened the space with two three-story glass galleries overlooking the docks along Ogden Slip, ideal for occupancy by restaurants. Inside, much of the original wood, brick and steel has been left exposed. High ceilings, open space, and bright colors provide a spatial environment well suited to a shopping and tourist atmosphere.

N5
CITYFRONT PLACE

400-480 North McClurg Court
Gelick Foran Associates, Ltd., 1992

This three-building complex contains 904 luxury rental units in a 39-story tower and two 12-story structures. A visual continuity is established in the three structures through the use of chamfered corners, red brick cladding and green-tinted window glass. The red brick also connects the complex to North Pier Terminal just to the east.

N6
CENTENNIAL FOUNTAIN

McClurg Court Esplanade at the River
Lohan Associates, 1989

Dirk Lohan, whose firm is responsible for the design of Cityfront Center, created this fountain commemorating the founding of the Metropolitan Water Reclamation District, the agency responsible for reversing the direction of the Chicago River. The fountain structure is a 125-foot long arc oriented toward the river with a circular pool and waterfall at its center. Periodically, water shoots out in a 210-foot arc over the Chicago River. Boaters alternate between delight and consternation at having to choose between waiting for the display or getting drenched by the shower.

N7
SHERATON CHICAGO

301 East North Water
Solomon Cordwell Buenz & Associates, 1992

In its dramatic setting on the riverfront, the Sheritan is wrapped with curving facades, calling attention to itself and offering its guests spectacular views.

N8
GLEACHER CENTER OF THE UNIVERSITY OF CHICAGO

450 North Cityfront Plaza Drive
Lohan Associates, 1994

A lecture and classroom center for the university's Graduate School of Business and non-degree students, the structure has a layered look, relating to Deconstructivism. The curved glass wall units appear to be anchored in place by a stepped, masonry screen pierced with complex, rectilinear windows. The focus of the design is the multi-story glazed wall section rising above the marquees of the double entrances. Lanterns along the summit reflect the marine character of the street lighting of the area.

GLEACHER CENTER OF THE UNIVERSITY OF CHICAGO

N9
NBC TOWER

454 North Columbus Drive
Skidmore, Owings, & Merrill, 1989

One of Chicago's most successful Post-Modern structures is this 38-story office tower with an adjoining 4-story radio and television facility. The entrances are adorned with intricate bronze metalwork. Adrian Smith, designer for SOM, chose to relate the structure to the 1920s buildings of the Magnificent Mile, especially to the Tribune Tower, just to the west. The NBC Tower rises with magnificent verticality, its windows grouped into vertical bands in the central east-west bays, which bow out, and on the north and south facades. Between continuous mullions, which carry the eye upward, recessed tinted-glass windows alternate with dark green pre-cast concrete spandrels resembling terra cotta. The building also recalls the architecture of the 1920s in the setbacks on the north and south, as well as irrational, "mock" flying buttresses near the crown, recalling those of the Tribune Tower. Limestone cladding is another visual connection to the 1920s, but unlike that of the earlier era, NBC's sheathing is a thin veneer bonded to huge precast-concrete panels. Crowning the design, above the NBC peacock logo, is a 120-foot spire.

N10
TIME-LIFE BUILDING

541 North Fairbanks Court (303 East Ohio)
Harry Weese & Associates, 1970

The 28-story Time-Life Building stands out against the cityscape because of its rich skin of Cor-ten steel and gold-tinted, solar reflecting glass. About ninety percent of the sun's ultraviolet rays are reflected back. The structure itself is a reinforced concrete skeleton three by seven bays, with piers spaced thirty feet apart in both directions. Clearly within the tradition of the Chicago School, the building reflects its structural system. The influence of Jacques Brownson's Daley Center is especially apparent. The lobby is set back to create covered walkways at the ground level. It is a very open, two-story space, with entrances on Ohio Street, Fairbanks Court, and Grand Avenue. Granite is used for the floor and walls of the lobby as well as for the sidewalk paving. An unusual feature is its double-deck elevators, incorporated here for the first time in America. The building was refurbished by Perkins & Will in 1990.

NBC TOWER

TIME-LIFE BUILDING

ONTERIE CENTRE

N11
ONTERIE CENTRE
446 East Ontario
Skidmore, Owings & Merrill, 1986

Onterie Centre, named for the two streets it faces, Ontario and Erie, is a 58-story office tower plus a 12-story structure and a 5-story triangular atrium, which connects the two. It has an unusual shape, flaring at the base. Its designers, Bruce Graham and Fazlur Khan, gave it a structure similar to that of the John Hancock; both buildings are diagonally braced tubes. Onterie Centre, however, is of reinforced concrete rather than steel, and instead of large steel diagonal members crossing window areas, in the Onterie certain window areas are filled in with concrete panels, producing the zig-zag effect. A tile wall mural in the lobby is dedicated to the memory of Fazlur Khan, who died in 1982, shortly before the building's groundbreaking.

N12
401 EAST ONTARIO
Nagle/Hartray & Associates, 1990

Triangular bays give a corrugated appearance to the walls of this 50-story apartment structure. In the corner units, living rooms are set at 45-degree angles, giving views in three directions. The building features retail space, parking, artists' studios, and on top a two-story recreation area.

N13
MCCLURG COURT CENTER
333 East Ontario
Solomon, Cordwell & Buenz, 1971-2

The slender 45-story apartment towers, at right angles to each other, have rounded corners, continuous mullions, and sheathing of dark tinted glass. When they were built, the towers provided quite a contrast to the cityscape of the south part of Streeterville, which was primarily that of warehouses and aging office buildings. In fact, it was not easy originally filling the 1,075 apartments, in spite of many perks: a movie theater, fitness center, shops and offices. The McClurg Center pioneered in paving the way for future development, and today the apartments are in much demand.

PRENTICE WOMEN'S HOSPITAL AND MATERNITY CENTER

N14
CBS BUILDING
630 North McClurg Ct.
Rebori, Wentworth, Dewey & McCormick, 1924

This industrial-type building was originally the Chicago Riding Club.

N15
237 EAST ONTARIO
(Formerly the Museum of Contemporary Art)
Anonymous Architect, 1915; Remodeling: Brenner, Danforth & Rockwell, 1967, followed by remodeling, Booth, Nagle & Hartray, 1979

This functional and aesthetically pleasing building was formerly used by *Playboy Magazine*, until 1967 when it was remodeled and opened as the Museum of Contemporary Art.

N16
ARTS CLUB
211 East Ontario
Vinci/Hamp Architects, 1997

When the former home of the Arts Club was demolished, the club decided to build their own structure, and the sale of a Brancusi sculpture to the Chicago Art Institute gave them funds to proceed. John Vinci, known primarily as a restoration architect, designed a structure so restrained that one might visually pass it by unless you're looking specifically for it. The glazed entrance, however, draws one in to a handsomely arranged interior, the focus of which is the restored Mies van der Rohe staircase removed from its former site and beautifully installed here.

N17
LAKE SHORE PLACE
(Formerly the American Furniture Mart)
680 North Lake Shore Drive
Henry Raeder & George Nimmons (east end), 1922-24; George Nimmons & Max Dunning (west end), 1925-26; Adaptive Reuse: Fujikawa, Conterato, & Lohan with Larocca Associates, 1979 and Lohan Associates, 1982-84

The former American Furniture Mart, later known as the 666 North Lake Shore Drive Building, is today known as 680 North Lake Shore Place. The massive structure, which has beautiful Gothic details, was once the largest building in the world and housed exhibition space for furniture manufacturers and dealers. It was converted to condominiums in 1980 and then into apartments in 1985. The 16-story main part of the building, on the east side, was built in 1924 of reinforced concrete, while the 20-story west portion is steel-framed and is surmounted by a blue campanile tower, which has become a landmark of the area.

N18
PRENTICE WOMEN'S HOSPITAL AND MATERNITY CENTER
333 East Superior
Bertrand Goldberg Associates, 1975

Goldberg's architecture is dramatic and sculptural. Here a seven-story quatrefoil tower springs gracefully from its four-story rectangular base. In the tower plan, four rounded shapes containing patient's rooms radiate from a central core, in which utilities and nursing stations are located. The oval windows appear to be punched in the bulging, organic concrete surfaces.

N19
TARRY MEDICAL RESEARCH AND EDUCATION BUILDING
300 East Superior
Perkins & Will Partnership, 1990

This modern skyscraper continues Northwestern University's Collegiate Gothic tradition.

N20
AMERICAN DENTAL ASSOCIATION BUILDING
211 East Chicago Avenue
Graham, Anderson, Probst, & White, 1965

This svelte, 23-story building has closely-spaced peripheral concrete piers, which carry the eye dramatically upward. The core of the structure provides much of its strength as well as holding elevators, lavatories and other services.

N21
NORTHWESTERN UNIVERSITY, CHICAGO CAMPUS
Montgomery Ward Memorial Building, *303-11 East Chicago Avenue*
Levy Mayer Hall, School of Law, *339 East Chicago Avenue*
Wieboldt Hall of Commerce, *357 East Chicago Avenue*
James Gamble Rogers, 1926-27

Northwestern University's choice of Gothic was probably related to the tradition it had already established on its primary campus in Evanston. Gothic campuses were especially popular in the 1920s, and many were being constructed across the U.S. Rogers had established a reputation as part of this movement.

N22
ARTHUR RUBLOFF BUILDING
750 North Lake Shore Drive
Holabird & Root, 1984

When this building was proposed, it was to be an addition to the Northwestern Law School. The program became more complicated, however, when the American Bar Association decided to move to the site on the Northwestern campus. Gerald Horn of Holabird & Root designed a twelve-story office building for the bar association and a four-story structure for the law school, both connected to each other and to an older Northwestern building by a 4-story glazed atrium structure. The complex structure was named after Rubloff, who donated $5 million to its erection.

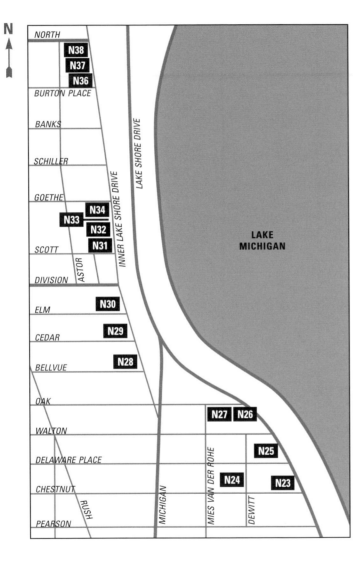

N23
860-880 NORTH LAKE SHORE DRIVE

N24
860 DEWITT APARTMENTS

N25
900-910 NORTH LAKE SHORE DRIVE

N26
999 NORTH LAKE SHORE DRIVE

N27
EAST LAKE SHORE DRIVE

N28
BRYAN LATHROP RESIDENCE
120 East Bellevue

N29
1100 NORTH LAKE SHORE DRIVE

N30
1130 NORTH LAKE SHORE DRIVE

N31
CARL CONSTANTINE HEISEN RESIDENCE
1250 North Lake Shore Drive

N32
MASON BRAYMAN STARRING RESIDENCE
1254 North Lake Shore Drive

N33
ARTHUR T. ALDIS RESIDENCE
1258 North Lake Shore Drive

N34
WARREN D. ROCKWELL RESIDENCE
1260 North Lake Shore Drive

N35
1418 NORTH LAKE SHORE DRIVE

N36
INTERNATIONAL COLLEGE OF SURGEONS
1516 North Lake Shore Drive

N37
INTERNATIONAL COLLEGE OF SURGEONS MUSEUM
1524 North Lake Shore Drive

N38
POLISH CONSULATE
1530 North Lake Shore Drive

LAKE SHORE DRIVE

After the Chicago Fire of 1871, debris was used to fill in some of the swampy land on the lakefront, and it was not long before residences were built. The greatest impetus to development occurred, however, after 1882, when Potter Palmer built his imposing mansion on the 1300 block. In the decade that followed, according to Thomas Tallmadge, land values rose from $160 per front foot to $800. Values have continued to rise ever since. Few mansions have escaped the wrecking ball. As property values rose, so did taxes: thus the offers from developers were attractive. The transformation of Lake Shore Drive by developers has gone on for a hundred years, with varying quality.

NORTH

N23
860-880 NORTH LAKE SHORE DRIVE
Ludwig Mies van der Rohe, 1949-51

860-880 NORTH LAKE DRIVE

When these apartment towers were constructed, they received international attention. Never before had glass skyscrapers of such stark and pristine form been built. Their construction set a trend for a new , sophisticated life-style, and architecturally they set a trend providing the ultimate model for a new generation of skyscrapers. The buildings are set perpendicular to each other to provide residents with maximum views of the lake. Identical in size, they are 26-story and 105 feet by 63 feet in plan. The facades are divided into three and five bays with columns every 21 feet. Glass-enclosed lobbies, set back from the peripheral columns, are furnished with Barcelona chairs and tables. The towers spring from a continuous travertine base, which serves as lobby floor and exterior patio. The construction cost of $10.38 per square foot was well below the conventional rate.

Mies expresses here the honesty of his structural system. One sees the piers rising from the ground to summit, but also the I-section mullions, which carry the eye in an unbroken sweep from the second floor upward. Although the steel of the structure itself is covered with concrete fire-proofing, Mies applied additional steel over the fireproofing so the building exhibits the material of which it was built.

N24
860 DEWITT APARTMENTS
(Chestnut-DeWitt Apartments)
Skidmore, Owings & Merrill, 1963

Fazlur Khan, one of the most brilliant structural engineers of this century, devised and used for the first time in this very slender 43-story apartment tower a new structural system of great strength, economy and practicality. The building is not carried on a skeleton; instead, its reinforced concrete walls are load-bearing screens, monolithically connected so that they form a very rigid, vertical, rectangular tube. The design team, which included Bruce Graham and Myron Goldsmith along with Khan, went on to design many other tubular structures, such as the Hancock Building and the Sears Tower.

N25
900-910 NORTH LAKE SHORE DRIVE
Ludwig Mies van der Rohe, 1953-56

Originally called 900 Esplanade, these two structures, which appear dark because of their tinted glass, are the same height as the two apartment buildings to the south, but two additional floors were squeezed in, giving each 28 stories. Instead of steel, like that of their neighbors at 860-880, their skeleton is a flat-slab concrete frame.

N26
999 NORTH LAKE SHORE DRIVE
Marshall & Fox, 1912
Typical of the work of Benjamin Marshall, this cooperative apartment building has red brick walls trimmed with limestone, and a strongly French flavor with a Second Empire mansard roof.

N27
EAST LAKE SHORE DRIVE

229 East Lake Shore Drive, Fugard & Knapp, 1919
219 East Lake Shore Drive, Fugard & Knapp, 1922
209 E. Lake Shore Drive, Marshall & Fox, 1924
199 East Lake Shore Drive, Marshall & Fox, 1915
Mayfair Regent Hotel, *181 East Lake Shore Drive,*
Fugard & Knapp, 1924
Drake Tower Apartments, *179 East Lake Shore
Drive,* Benjamin H. Marshall, 1929

These apartment buildings, along with 999 North Lake Shore Drive, which wraps the corner where East and North Lake Shore Drive meet, form a visual unity. Design elements from French and English historical styles blend harmoniously. The original apartments were very large by today's standards, although many have since been broken into smaller units. These buildings offer luxury living at prestigious addresses to residents who want spaciousness without the responsibility of a house.

N28
BRYAN LATHROP RESIDENCE

120 East Bellevue
McKim, Mead & White, 1891-92

Bryan Lathrop, a wealthy Chicago real estate investor, chose his friend Charles F. McKim of the prestigious Boston architectural firm, McKim, Mead & White, to design his home. The three-story, 23-room mansion is in the Federal Revival style, a version of late Georgian architecture, popular in America around 1800.

Characteristic of the style are the rounded, bulging bays at either side, the shallow relieving arches over the ground-story openings, and delicate carving of details. The brick is laid in Flemish bond (that is, alternating brick stretchers and headers on each course). In 1923 the structure was purchased by a women's organization, the Fortnightly Club.

N29
1100 NORTH LAKE SHORE DRIVE
Harry Weese & Associates, 1980

This 40-story condominium building at the corner of Lake Shore Drive and Cedar Street is a reinforced concrete structure with bronze-tinted glass windows. All of its seventy-six units are at least 2,000 square feet, and half of them are 2-story.

N30
1130 NORTH LAKE SHORE DRIVE
Howard Van Doren Shaw, 1911

Already in the first and second decade of the twentieth century, apartment buildings were replacing residences built only ten to fifteen years earlier. This Tudor revival building was designed with spacious apartments, one per floor.

BRYAN LATHROP RESIDENCE

ARTHUR T. ALDIS RESIDENCE

1418 NORTH LAKE SHORE DRIVE

N31
CARL CONSTANTINE HEISEN RESIDENCE
1250 North Lake Shore Drive
Frank B. Abbott, 1890-91

Heisen was a German who came to Chicago and made a fortune in real estate. His house has been joined to its neighbor, the Starring house on the north, to form four expensive dwellings.

N32
MASON BRAYMAN STARRING RESIDENCE
1254 North Lake Shore Drive
Gustav Hallberg, 1889

Compare this to the Heisen house next door, built by Frank Abbott at approximately the same time. Both houses are in the Romanesque revival style. Typically, they have rounded arches, rusticated stone walls, squat colonnettes, massive walls, and towers.

N33
ARTHUR T. ALDIS RESIDENCE
1258 North Lake Shore Drive
Holabird & Roche, 1895

Holabird & Roche, who were very active at this time building some of Chicago's most progressive skyscrapers, built this Venetian Gothic mansion. The 3-story house, faced with red brick and limestone trim, has a *piano nobile* fronted by a stone balcony.

N34
WARREN D. ROCKWELL RESIDENCE
1260 North Lake Shore Drive
Holabird & Roche, 1910

By the beginning of the twentieth century, the Georgian style was thought to be extremely fashionable.

N35
1418 NORTH LAKE SHORE DRIVE
Solomon, Cordwell, Buenz & Associates, 1983

John Buenz designed this 29-story building on a narrow site, which had formerly been occupied by a single-family mansion. The sliver-like, 44-foot wide tower has only one apartment unit per floor. An angled glass facade, having a pleated effect, juts out twelve feet in order to provide panoramic views and greater interior floor space for the apartments without blocking the views of neighboring buildings.

N36
INTERNATIONAL COLLEGE OF SURGEONS

(Edward T. Blair Residence)
1516 North Lake Shore Drive
McKim, Mead & White, 1912

One of only three residences built in Chicago by this prominent Boston architectural firm, this restrained Renaissance-style home set the stage for the two later homes built to the north.

N37
INTERNATIONAL COLLEGE OF SURGEONS MUSEUM

(Eleanor Robinson Countiss Residence)
1524 North Lake Shore Drive
Howard Van Doren Shaw, 1918

Uniting the classical homes on either side, the Countiss residence is the largest of the three. Supposedly, it was inspired by the *Petit Trionon* at Versailles, but it is taller, with four stories. Fluted pilasters span the upper three stories.

N38
POLISH CONSULATE

(Bernard A. Eckhart Residence)
1530 North Lake Shore Drive
Benjamin H. Marshall, 1916

Two large classic Palladian windows grace the second story of this beautifully-proportioned 4-story home. The upper story is adorned with delicate Renaissance-style ornament

POLISH CONSULATE

INTERNATIONAL COLLEGE OF SURGEONS MUSEUM AND THE POLISH CONSULATE

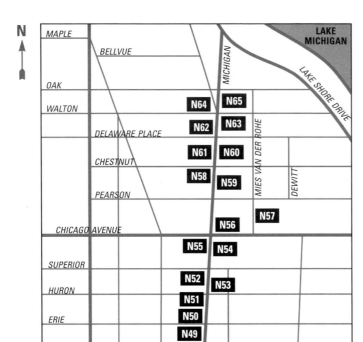

N39
WRIGLEY BUILDING
400 North Michigan

N40
EQUITABLE BUILDING
401 North Michigan

N41
TRIBUNE TOWER
435 North Michigan

N42
HOTEL
INTER-CONTINENTAL
505 North Michigan

N43
520 NORTH MICHIGAN

N44
MARRIOTT HOTEL
540 North Michigan

N45
JACQUES BUILDING
543 North Michigan

N46
600 NORTH MICHIGAN

N47
FIRST NATIONAL BANK OF
CHICAGO
605 North Michigan

N48
WOMAN'S ATHLETIC CLUB
626 North Michigan

N49
CRATE & BARREL
646 North Michigan

N50
TERRA MUSEUM OF AMERICAN
ART
666 North Michigan Avenue

N51
CITY PLACE
676 North Michigan

N52
CHICAGO PLACE
700 North Michigan

N53
ALLERTON HOTEL
701 North Michigan

N54
OLYMPIA CENTRE
737 North Michigan

N55
SHOPPING COMPLEX
744 North Michigan

N56
CHICAGO WATER TOWER AND
PUMPING STATION
Chicago Avenue and Michigan

N57
MUSEUM OF CONTEMPORARY
ART
220 East Chicago Avenue

N58
840 NORTH MICHIGAN

N59
WATER TOWER PLACE
845 North Michigan

N60
JOHN HANCOCK CENTER
875 North Michigan

N61
FOURTH PRESBYTERIAN CHURCH
866 North Michigan

N62
900 NORTH MICHIGAN

N63
PALMOLIVE BUILDING
919 North Michigan

N64
ONE MAGNIFICENT MILE
940-980 North Michigan

N65
DRAKE HOTEL
140 East Walton

MAGNIFICENT MILE

Michigan Avenue became an elegant commercial thoroughfare in the 1920s, following the opening of the 220-foot, double leaf bascule bridge, which connected the Loop proper with the north extension of the street. In the early 1920s, revival styles dominated in such structures as the Wrigley Building and the Tribune Tower, but later in the decade, the new French style, Art Deco, took precedence. The character of the street has changed dramatically again since the 1960s, when a series of skyscrapers of a much greater scale were constructed, dwarfing many of the older buildings. Today the street is the most fashionable in the city, a thriving thoroughfare of elegant vertical shopping centers, office towers, rental and condominium complexes and expensive hotels.

Michigan Avenue from the River to Oak Street

NORTH

WRIGLEY BUILDING

EQUITABLE BUILDING

N39
WRIGLEY BUILDING
400 North Michigan
Graham, Anderson, Probst, & White, 1919-24

The corporate offices of the Wrigley chewing gum company have a magnificent setting on the banks of the river and at the entrance to the Magnificent Mile. The Wrigley is actually two buildings, one completed in 1921 and the other in 1924, with passageways connecting the structures at the third and fourteenth floors. The inspiration for the Spanish Renaissance design was a tower added to the cathedral of Seville in the sixteenth century. The taller portion of the Wrigley to the south exhibits a clock with four dials and at its summit a round, colonnaded cupola. Delicate Renaissance-style ornament in shallow relief flows profusely over the surfaces. The whole is covered with white terra cotta, molded with Renaissance style designs. At night the structure is a brilliantly floodlit symbol of the city.

N40
EQUITABLE BUILDING
401 North Michigan
Skidmore, Owings & Merrill, 1965

The 35-story Equitable Building clearly expresses its skeleton structure. The gray-green aluminum sheathing of the piers actually takes the form of hollow box-shaped units containing conduits for hot and cold air. the spandrels are of gray granite. Each bay is filled with four bronze-tinted windows. For variety the outer two are narrower than the inner two. In front of the Equitable is Pioneer Court, by Graham, Anderson, Probst and White, commemorating 25 Chicago pioneers whose names are in bronze letters around a travertine fountain. McCormick's Reaper Works were about 150 feet to the east.

N41
TRIBUNE TOWER
435 North Michigan
Howells & Hood, 1923-25

The 34-story Gothic revival Tribune Tower was the chosen design in an international competition in 1922. Col. Robert R. McCormick, owner of the newspaper, announced that $100,000 in prizes would be given for a design for "the world's most beautiful office building." Ten American architects received special invitations to participate and $2000 honorariums. Hints appeared in the paper that Gothic was the preferred style, although not all the entrants learned this. One announcement claimed that the judges liked Cass Gilbert's Woolworth Building in New York, a Gothic tower. 264 applications were submitted representing 23 countries. Some of the European entries were extremely modern, especially that of Walter Gropius of Germany. The jury, composed of Alfred Granger, president of the Chicago Chapter of the AIA, and four Tribune men, selected the Gothic design of John Mead Howells and Raymond Hood of New York. Second prize in the competition went to Eliel Saarinen of Finland, whose stepped-back vertical design became influential even though it was never built.

The structure of the Tribune is a steel frame, sheathed in Indiana limestone. Its tower, which includes a ring of eight flying buttresses, was inspired by the Tour de Beurre of the Rouen Cathedral. The more progressive architects of the day questioned the structural honesty of imitating a medieval structural system in a modern skyscraper. While the Tribune called the building "a symphony in white," Louis Sullivan spoke bitterly against it, comparing the tower to a "monstrous, eight-legged spider."

The building's three-story arched entrance is beautifully proportioned. Embedded in the lower walls to either side are stone relics "pirated" from famous monuments of the world—the Arc de Triomphe, the Taj Mahal, the Great Wall of China, the Parthenon, Westminster Abbey. Just to the north of the main tower is the four-story Gothic annex, with a statue of Nathan Hale in a small court.

N42

HOTEL INTER-CONTINENTAL
505 North Michigan
South Tower, Walter W. Ahlschlager, 1929: North Tower, Quinn & Christensen, 1961; Restoration, Harry Weese & Associates, 1989

Once the tallest building in Chicago, the former Medinah Athletic Club has been renovated to recreate much of its original splendor. Now the 348-room Hotel Inter-Continental Chicago, one can experience here a sort of calliope of decorative styles, including Moorish, Spanish, Italianate, Assyrian, Gothic and much more, with ornamental detail carved or cast in profusion. A beautiful Olympic-sized pool on the 14th floor is lined with Spanish majolica tiles. Atop the 42-story south tower, part of the original structure, is a gold dome and minaret. The north tower now houses the less expensive, 517-room Forum Hotel, also owned by the Inter-Continental.

N43
520 NORTH MICHIGAN
(Formerly McGraw-Hill Building)
Thielbar & Fugard, 1929

The shallow incised ornament on this limestone-clad Art Deco building is of exceptional quality.

N44
MARRIOTT HOTEL
540 North Michigan
Harry Weese & Associates, 1978

This massive cubic structure provides no visual interest on its exterior and is atypical of Weese's work.

TRIBUNE TOWER

CRATE & BARREL

N45
JACQUES BUILDING
543 North Michigan
Philip B. Maher, 1929

The sculptural panels above the entrance reflect the building's original function as a store for expensive women's clothing. Maher's style reflects his influence from the Art Deco, which was at its height in Paris in 1925-6 when he was studying there.

N46
600 NORTH MICHIGAN
Beyer Blinder Belle of New York, 1997

A combination shopping and multi-cinema structure, the building calls attention to itself through its vertical cylindrical corner units, bright terra cotta panels on the exterior and its openness to the street. The geometry of its profile, due especially to the rectangular cinema structure on top, weakens the appearance of the whole. The structure has aroused much controversy, because it required the demolition of a fine building housing the Arts Club and because its character is in opposition to the elegant structures nearby.

N47
FIRST NATIONAL BANK OF CHICAGO
(Lake Shore Trust Building)
605 North Michigan
Marshall & Fox, 1922; Renovation and addition, Perkins & Will, 1982

Huge Corinthian columns of elegant proportions adorn this classical temple design.

N48
WOMAN'S ATHLETIC CLUB
626 North Michigan
Philip B. Maher, 1928

One of Philip Maher's most impressive designs, this French-style structure is clad in limestone with delicate ornament, large arched windows, quoins, pilasters, and a mansard roof.

N49
CRATE & BARREL
646 North Michigan
Solomon Cordwell Buenz & Associates, 1990

One of the more recent additions to Michigan Avenue is this sleek, streamlined Post-Modern glass and white aluminum structure. There are many references to the International Style of Le Corbusier or Mendelsohn: rounded corners, steamship-type railings and smooth white surfaces. The owners of this innovative, 5-story housewares store sought to entice shoppers by making the merchandise visible on the exterior; hence glass walls and a highly lit interior. The glass-enclosed rotunda at the corner serves as the circulation system.

N50
TERRA MUSEUM OF AMERICAN ART
666 North Michigan Avenue
Booth/Hansen & Associates, 1987
664 North Michigan Avenue (Formerly the Farwell Building)
Philip B. Maher, 1927

Booth/Hansen gutted the interior space of two existing structures and joined them with a new glass-walled central core housing the circulation system and entrance. The interior is suitably spacious and effectively designed for moderate-sized exhibitions.

N51
CITY PLACE
676 North Michigan
Loebl, Schlossman & Hackl, 1990

The 40-story City Place combines a three-story base sheathed in shades of red granite; a 24-story Hyatt Regency Hotel with red vertical bands and pink spandrels; and a 13-story office unit with curved setbacks and a large arch on top. The retail entrance is on Michigan, while the others are on Huron.

N52
CHICAGO PLACE
700 North Michigan
Skidmore, Owings & Merrill, 1990 (retail); Solomon Cordwell Buenz & Associates, (condo tower)

The large arched window crowning the facade, the rounded corners, and the lively color of this 8-level retail complex provide it with a feeling of gaiety suitable for a shopping facility. SOM partner-designer Bruce Graham claims to have been inspired by Louis Sullivan's Carson Pirie Scott, which also has the rounded corner and horizontal windows.

CHICAGO PLACE

CHICAGO WATER TOWER AND PUMPING STATION

N53
ALLERTON HOTEL
701 North Michigan
Murgatroyd & Ogden, 1924

Originally called Allerton House, this Italian Renaissance style "club hotel" was part of a New York chain. In 1924, it was the first hotel of its type on North Michigan Avenue.

N54
OLYMPIA CENTRE
737 North Michigan
Skidmore, Owings & Merrill, 1983-86

Adrian Smith designed Olympia Centre for an L-shaped lot which wraps around the 777 North Michigan building. One part of the structure with an entrance on Chicago Avenue is a 63-story, tapering concrete "tube" tower with offices from the fifth to the 22nd floor and condominiums on the top 39 stories. The second part of the structure is the four-story Nieman Marcus department store. A dramatic glass arch, 38 feet wide and 57 feet high, lined with stained glass, invites shoppers inside. The exterior walls are sheathed with alternating bands of rough and polished pink granite from Carrara, Italy.

N55
SHOPPING COMPLEX
744 North Michigan
Elkus Manfredi, 1997

Howard Elkus of Boston is responsible for this complex of shopping facilities developed by Thomas J. Klutznick. The individual client-oriented units appear as separate buildings in a variety of historically-inspired facades opening directly to the street.

N56
CHICAGO WATER TOWER AND PUMPING STATION
Chicago and Michigan Avenues
W.W. Boyington, 1866-70

Boyington, the most prolific Chicago architect of the time, enclosed an iron standpipe, 3 feet in diameter and 138 feet high, which served to equalize the water pressure in this Gothic structure of rusticated Joliet limestone. The castellated octagonal tower, surmounted by an iron cupola, rises from a square base with four identical elevations. Pointed arches, turrets, and slit-like windows emphasize the verticality. This and the Pumping Station next door miraculously survived the great Fire of 1871. The tower serves today as a Visitors' Center.

N57
MUSEUM OF CONTEMPORARY ART
220 East Chicago Avenue
Joseph Paul Kleihues, 1996

One of the largest contemporary art museums in the world, this new structure by a Berlin architect has sparked quite a controversy. Somewhat intimidating and fortress-like on the exterior, this boxy five-story structure is reached by 32 steps on the building's west side. The walls are clad in cold cast aluminum panels attached with round steel pins, surmounted on a base of Indiana limestone. The interior, however, is another story. A 55-foot atrium space extending through the building and high barrel-vaulted galleries provide spaciousness. Fish-shaped staircases are beautiful and dynamic, contrasting with some of the more static spaces. Finally, an exterior sculpture garden extends toward the lake.

N58
840 NORTH MICHIGAN
Lucien Lagrange & Associates, 1992

One of the newest towers on the avenue is this hotel-retail structure with a dramatic corner, complete with large arches, expanses of glass and flanking columns at the entrance. Rounded Second Empire roofs give the building a distinctly French flavor.

N59
WATER TOWER PLACE
845 North Michigan
Loebl Schlossman Bennett & Dart, 1976; Interiors by Warren Platner Associates

Water Tower Place is a two-part structure with a blocky, ten-story shopping mall and office building on Michigan Avenue and a 74-story tower, including the Ritz Carlton Hotel, entered at 150 East Pearson. When built, this was the world's tallest reinforced concrete building.

Although the shopping structure facing Michigan looks fortress-like because of its windowless, gray and white marble cladding, it is an open, glassy, plant-filled atrium on the interior. Edward Dart, designer of the structure, and Walter Platner Associates, in charge of interior design, have found the right combination to attract shoppers.

MUSEUM OF CONTEMPORARY ART

JOHN HANCOCK CENTER

900 NORTH MICHIGAN

N60
JOHN HANCOCK CENTER
875 North Michigan
Skidmore, Owings & Merrill, 1968

The tallest structure in the world when built, the Hancock reaches 1107 feet and 100 stories. Called "gutsy" by designer Bruce Graham, it has created much attention because of its inward-sloping walls and diagonal bracing. The inclined walls are rigidly joined to form a "tube", from which aluminum and glass curtain walls are hung. The tube system, developed largely by Skidmore engineering partner, the late Fazlur Khan, allowed for a 30% reduction in the amount of steel. Bold also is the wind-bracing system, a series of huge diagonal steel members each stretching over eighteen stories. The steel diagonals form triangular shapes which are extremely resistant to the stress of wind pressure.

The building is notable as well for its extremely multi-functional character with retail, parking, offices, restaurants, pool, health club, condominiums and apartments. The top floors of the building include an observation deck, a restaurant, bar and television station.

N61
FOURTH PRESBYTERIAN CHURCH
866 North Michigan
Ralph Adams Cram, 1914; Cloister, Howard Van Doren Shaw, 1914; Manse, Parish House, Blair Chapel, Howard Van Doren Shaw, 1925

In the best tradition of the Gothic revival, this small block provides an island of relief among the commercial structures on this busy street. Ralph Adams Cram was well-known in his day for having designed and built numerous Gothic revival churches and universities across the country and writing several architectural books. Howard Van Doren Shaw was a member of the local congregation and architect of numerous residences on the North Shore and in the Gold Coast.

N62
900 NORTH MICHIGAN
Kohn Pedersen Fox, 1989

This mixed-use superstructure includes a massive 8-story shopping facility facing Michigan and a 66-story tower with several setbacks entered from the side streets. The tower contains the Four Seasons Hotel, along with residential and office units; the shopping atrium's anchor store is Bloomingdale's. Structurally the design is a tube in which the lower floors are framed in steel, while the 36 upper stories are framed in concrete. The reinforcing rods of the concrete are joined to the steel columns at the 30th floor by thermal-fusion. The building has a complex facade treatment: flat classical elements, a circular "rose" window, and a palette of red, pink, brown and black granite; buff and gray limestone; and green and white marble; and reflective green-tinted glass. Four cupola-like lanterns on top dominate the profile.

N63
PALMOLIVE BUILDING

919 North Michigan
Holabird & Root, 1929

One of Chicago's finest Art Deco skyscrapers, the Palmolive emphasizes its verticality with a counterpoint of strongly projecting and recessed bands. Vertical ribbons of windows alternate with bands of openings, which appear punched in the limestone. A series of six, beautifully-proportioned setbacks are dramatic and elegant. The building has been successful since it was built: even during the depression, it maintained an occupancy-rate of 88.6%. The historic Lindbergh beacon rotated atop the structure for many years, although after the John Hancock building was built, the intense light bothered residents ,who complained. A less brilliant lamp serves today as a symbol.

N64
ONE MAGNIFICENT MILE

940-980 North Michigan
Skidmore, Owings & Merrill, 1983

ONE MAGNIFICENT MILE

One Magnificent Mile, developed by the Levy Organization, is one of the city's most expensive addresses. The first three floors are commercial; offices are from the fourth to the 19th stories; and the rest is condominium. A five-story hexagonal entrance pavilion with a sloping glazed roof provides an inviting access.

Bruce Graham and Fazlur Khan, who together had built many tube structures, created here a triple-tube of three hexagonal, reinforced concrete towers, rising 21, 49 and 58 stories. The exterior is finished in pink polished granite.

N65
DRAKE HOTEL

140 East Walton
Marshall & Fox, 1920

Marshall & Fox were masters in the design of grand, elegant interior spaces. One should enter the lobby, shopping corridors, and palm court to experience the spacious and beautiful proportions.

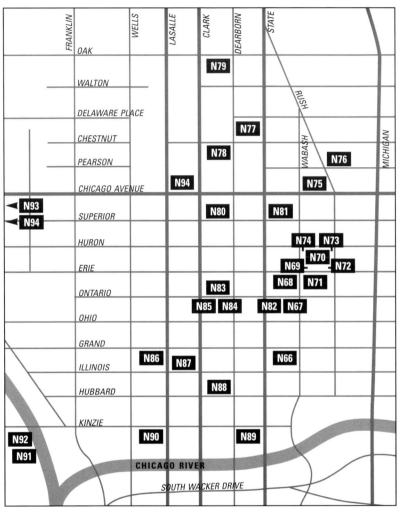

N66
AMERICAN MEDICAL
ASSOCIATION BUILDING
515 North State

N67
MEDINAH TEMPLE
600 North Wabash

N68
RANSOM R. CABLE
RESIDENCE
25 East Erie

N69
SAMUEL M. NICKERSON
RESIDENCE
40 East Erie

N70
JOHN B. MURPHY
MEMORIAL THEATER
50 East Erie

N71
AMERICAN COLLEGE OF
SURGEONS
HEADQUARTERS
55 East Erie

N72
ROBERT HALL MCCORMICK
RESIDENCE
660 North Rush

N73
EPISCOPAL DIOCESE
CHURCH CENTER
65 East Huron

N74
EPISCOPAL CATHEDRAL OF
ST. JAMES
65 East Huron

N75
HOTEL ST. BENEDICT'S
FLATS
42-50 East Chicago Avenue

N76
QUIGLEY SEMINARY AND
CHAPEL OF ST. JAMES
831 North Rush

N77
CHESTNUT PLACE
850 North State

N78
JOHN FEWKES TOWER
55 West Chestnut

N79
NEWBERRY LIBRARY
60 West Walton

N80
ASBURY PLACE
750 North Dearborn

N81
HOLY NAME CATHEDRAL
735 North State

N82
TREE STUDIOS
601-23 North State

N83
EXCALIBUR
632 North Dearborn

N84
COMMONWEALTH EDISON
SUB-STATION
600 North Dearborn

N85
HARD-ROCK CAFE
63 West Ontario

N86
ANTI-CRUELTY SOCIETY
157 West Grand

N87
108 WEST ILLINOIS

N88
COURTHOUSE PLACE
54 West Hubbard

N89
HARRY CARAY'S
33 West Kenzie

N90
350 NORTH LASALLE

N91
FULTON HOUSE
345 North Canal

N92
RIVER COTTAGES
357-65 North Canal

N93
MONTGOMERY WARD
WAREHOUSE BUILDINGS
*604, 619 West Chicago
Avenue*

N94
MONTGOMERY WARD
CORPORATE OFFICES
535 West Chicago Avenue

RIVER NORTH

River North is a district in transition. Early in its history, its easternmost streets were primarily residential. Chicago's wealthiest citizens built homes north of Grand along Rush, Wabash, State and Dearborn. Further west, factories and warehouses predominated. In recent years new businesses have moved in, warehouses have been converted to condominiums, a great variety of restaurants have been opened, apartment buildings and hotels have been built and the streets teem with people. The versatility of structures, functions and services makes the area one of the liveliest in the city.

NORTH

N66
AMERICAN MEDICAL ASSOCIATION BUILDING
515 North State,
Kenzo Tange, 1990

The first major American work of Japanese architect Kenzo Tange is this 30-story office building. The crystalline appearance of the sleek aluminum and glass curtain wall tower is enhanced with a visual focus on a four-story hole, or negative space, near the summit of its sharpest corner. A smaller tower is planned as a companion building to the south.

N67
MEDINAH TEMPLE
600 North Wabash
Huehl & Schmid, 1912

A lodge for the Shriners, this block-sized, four-story building contains an auditorium used for conventions, circuses, and drills. A large onion-shaped dome rises from the roof and smaller pointed domes crown two corners of the structure. Exotic Arabic-style ornament abounds in metal grills, textured brick and tilework, and stained glass windows.

N68
RANSOM R. CABLE RESIDENCE
(Driehaus Financial Services)
25 East Erie
Cobb & Frost, 1886

The Romanesque revival was one of the most fashionable and characteristic styles of Chicago in the 1880s. No doubt influenced by H.H. Richardson, who was erecting three other Romanesque buildings in Chicago at the time, Cobb & Frost's Cable house is of light orange Kasota limestone with battered foundations, large round arches, a corner entrance and typical vegetative ornament.

N69
SAMUEL M. NICKERSON RESIDENCE
(R.H. Love Galleries)
40 East Erie Street
Burling & Whitehouse, 1883

Near the end of his career, Burling, Chicago's second architect, having come here in 1843 from New York State, designed this mansion for Samuel Nickerson, the first president of First National Bank. The three-story structure, which cost a half million dollars to build (a huge sum for the time) is constructed of sand-stone ashlar with Italian Renaissance frieze, cornice and horizontal banding. The interior is richly designed with marble and parquet floors, onyx columns, and profuse ornament. An addition was built in 1901 by George Maher.

N70
JOHN B. MURPHY MEMORIAL THEATER
50 East Erie
Marshall & Fox, 1923-26

This little architectural gem, out of character for the area, has a beautifully-proportioned colonnaded portico, a curving staircase and bronze entrance door by Tiffany Studios. Modeled on the *Chapelle de Notre-Dame de Consolation* in Paris, it serves as an auditorium and library. Built on land that once belonged to the Nickersons, it was given to the American College of Surgeons.

N71
AMERICAN COLLEGE OF SURGEONS HEADQUARTERS
55 East Erie
Skidmore, Owings & Merrill, 1963; Addition: Graham, Anderson, Probst & White, 1983

Built of porous reinforced concrete with glass walls, this small structure has refined proportions and an elegance in its simplicity.

N72
ROBERT HALL MCCORMICK RESIDENCE
(Chez Paul)
660 North Rush
Anonymous Architect, 1875

This limestone Italianate house was built for the brother of Cyrus McCormick (of reaper fame) in an area nicknamed "McCormickville". Cyrus McCormick and their father Leander McCormick lived nearby. The remnants of the L. Hamilton McCormick house, incorporated now within the structure of Lawry's Restaurant, can be seen above its roofline across the street at 631 N. Rush.

HOTEL ST. BENEDICT'S FLATS

N73
EPISCOPAL DIOCESE CHURCH CENTER
65 East Huron
James W. Hammond & Peter Roesch, 1969

Strongly influenced by Mies Van der Rohe and the International Style, this structure is classic and pristine. The building's piers are at the periphery, allowing 45-foot column-free clear spans, and the two end walls are cantilevered beyond the piers. An underground tunnel connects this structure with the cathedral.

N74
EPISCOPAL CATHEDRAL OF ST. JAMES
65 East Huron
Burling & Adler, 1875; Tower remaining from pre-Fire church, Burling & Bacchus, 1856; Chapel, Cram, Goodhue & Ferguson, 1913

After the Fire, which left only the tower of the 1856 church, the building was reconstructed of Joliet rock-faced limestone in the original Victorian Gothic style. A 1984 restoration by Holabird & Root revealed a magnificent Art-and-Crafts interior under many coats of paint. The walls and beams are covered in colorful stencilled designs produced in1888 by Edward Neville Stent of New York.

N75
HOTEL ST. BENEDICT'S FLATS
42-50 East Chicago Avenue
James J. Egan, 1882

Typical of the Victorian era, these eclectic apartments have Gothic and Queen Anne details as well as "French-style" mansard roofs.

N76
QUIGLEY SEMINARY AND CHAPEL OF ST JAMES
831 North Rush Street
Zachary T. Davis, 1919

Built just after World War I, in a period when revivalism was rampant, this structure is a study in the French Gothic style. It includes a chapel inspired by *Sainte-Chapelle* in Paris, where the French royalty worshiped since the fourteenth century.

N77
CHESTNUT PLACE
850 North State
Weese, Seegers, Hickey, Weese, 1982

This 15-sided, 30-story apartment structure is visually notable for its vertical bands of contrasting brick and punched windows. But more unusual is its private lobby, painted by New York *trompe l'oeil* artist Richard Hass to imitate an Italian Romanesque courtyard, with a blue sky above and with geometric patterning on the walls and floor adapted from those of *San Miniato al Monte* in Florence.

N78
JOHN FEWKES TOWER
55 West Chestnut
Harry Weese & Associates, 1967

Trapezoidal bay windows and chamfered corners distinguish this 30-story apartment tower.

N79
NEWBERRY LIBRARY
60 West Walton
Henry Ives Cobb, 1892; Addition to north, Harry Weese, 1982

Henry Ives Cobb, trained at Massachusetts Institute of Technology and Harvard, had a strong preference for the Romanesque style. Cobb received the commission for the Newberry Library in 1888 with the understanding that he would resign his partnership with Charles Frost. The long facade of pink granite from Milford, Connecticut is divided into five dignified, projecting and receding units. The central triple-arched portal of beautiful proportions was influenced by the twelfth century church at Saint-Gilles-du-Gard in southern France. Cobb picked up on some of the Moorish rhythms typical of Romanesque in southern France and Spain.

N80
ASBURY PLACE
750 North Dearborn
George Schipporeit, 1981

This angular, reinforced concrete high rise apartment structure has a complex geometric layout throughout, with scarcely any rectangular spaces, but the shapes are well designed and give the apartments interest as well as maximum views of the city.

NEWBERRY LIBRARY

EXCALIBUR

N81
HOLY NAME CATHEDRAL

735 North State

Patrick C. Kelly, 1874-5; Renovations: Henry J. Schlacks, 1915; Alfred F. Pashley and James Willet, 1893; and C.F. Murphy, 1969

Patrick Kelly of Brooklyn is responsible for this Victorian Gothic cruciform church of limestone ashlar construction. It replaced an earlier Gothic church destroyed in the Chicago Fire of 1871.

N82
TREE STUDIOS

601-23 North State

Hill and Woltersdorf, 1894; Additions at *12 E. Ohio and 7 E. Ontario*, Woltersdorf and Bernhard, 1912-13

Judge Lambert Tree, whose Peabody and Stearns home was next door where the Medinah Temple now stands, constructed these studios for artists above street level shops. The light, airy apartments with high ceilings still attract artists today. A rear court garden is hidden from view.

N83
EXCALIBUR

(Formerly Chicago Public Library)
632 North Dearborn
Cobb & Frost, 1892

Cobb, who was very much influenced by H.H. Richardson, created one of Chicago's best examples of the Romanesque style. The fortress-like structure has heavy rusticated walls of Aberdeen red granite with an entrance nestled between two rounded towers with conical roofs. The building has served several purposes since the historical society moved out in 1932. At one time it housed the school called the Chicago Bauhaus, headed by Lazlo Moholy-Nagy, and in recent years, the Limelight Club followed by the Excalibur.

N84
COMMONWEALTH EDISON SUB-STATION
600 North Dearborn
Tigerman, Fugman, McCurry, 1989

Tigerman seems to have taken the concept of contexturalism seriously, for he adopted the Georgian style to blend with his own Hard Rock Cafe next door, and in addition, incorporated elements from the previous Georgian style substation. Very anti-Georgian, however, is the scale of the exaggerated details: the Palladian window, the pedimented temple shapes, and the massive stringcourses. Perhaps the heavy-handedness was suggested by the machinery within.

N85
HARD ROCK CAFE
63 West Ontario
Tigerman, Fugman, McCurry, 1986

Tigerman claimed to have picked up the cornice lines, the Palladian windows and other motifs from the Commonwealth Edison substation next door; and what he arrived at, in his own words, was a "Neo-Georgian orangery". Little did he know that the sub-station next door would be torn down, but that only provided him with another opportunity. Tigerman has also designed Hard Rocks for Houston, Honolulu and New Orleans.

N86
ANTI-CRUELTY SOCIETY
157 West Grand
Leon Stanhope, 1935; Addition: Stanley Tigerman & Associates, 1982

Tigerman's addition is an interesting Post-modern design. This pet adoption facility is unpretentious in its use of aluminum siding and sash windows, and whimsical in its play of flamboyant baroque and Palladian shapes, including a high false front with its illusion of cutout layered planes of solids and voids. Referred to as the "doggie-in-the-window" building, the shape of the cutout on the roof seems to refer to a dog food can key, while the window shapes flanking the entrance may refer to the jowls of a basset hound.

COMMONWEALTH EDISON SUB-STATION

ANTI-CRUELTY SOCIETY

COURTHOUSE PLACE

N87
108 WEST ILLINOIS

(Formerly Grommes & Ullrich Warehouse)
Richard E. Schmidt, 1901

Hugh Garden, working for Schmidt, was the designer for this liquor company's office warehouse. The building's strong horizontality, expressed through wide windows, continuous, unbroken spandrels, and projecting horizontal brick banding between windows, identify it as an example of the Prairie School.

N88
COURTHOUSE PLACE

(Cook County Criminal Courts Building)
54 West Hubbard
Otto Matz, 1892; Renovation, Solomon Cordwell Buenz & Associates, 1986

This six-story, Romanesque revival building of rusticated Bedford limestone has witnessed some of the famous trials of Clarence Darrow, as well as the questioning of Al Capone and the trials of gangsters of the depression days. The building's heavy walls appropriately represent power and authority. Above the entrance is a figure of Justice with a sword and scales. Interestingly, the site was featured in a 1928 play, *The Front Page*, by Ben Hecht and Charles MacArthur, about gangsters and newspaper editors in Chicago.

N89
HARRY CARAY'S

(Chicago Varnish Company)
33 West Kinzie
Henry Ives Cobb, 1895

This flamboyant structure in the Flemish Renaissance style was once owned by the Chicago Varnish Company, which made coatings for railroad equipment as well as furniture.

N90
350 NORTH LASALLE

Loebl, Schlossman & Hackl, 1990

Developed by a law firm and designed for law offices, this 15-story, reinforced concrete building was erected on a thin, long- sloping site. Its facades are faced with red brick in a grid pattern, and bays are filled with green glass.

N91
FULTON HOUSE
345 North Canal
Frank Abbott, 1908; Adaptive re-use by Harry Weese & Associates, 1979-81

This 16-story pink brick structure was originally built in 1908 as the North American Cold Storage warehouse with reinforced concrete, largely windowless walls 12 to 16 inches thick. In order to convert the building to living spaces, Harry Weese had to create 500 windows in the immense walls. One hundred four loft-style condominiums were created, and the structure was renamed Fulton House.

N92
RIVER COTTAGES
357-65 North Canal
Harry Weese & Associates, 1990

Perhaps inspired by ships' sails, these four tall, narrow townhouses hug the banks of the North Branch of the Chicago River. The end facades form isosceles triangles, in which the long sides , which descends sharply toward the river. The shorter units also have triangular tubular bracing above their roofs.

N93
MONTGOMERY WARD WAREHOUSE BUILDINGS
604 West Chicago Avenue: Warehouse building, Schmidt, Garden & Martin, 1906-08
619 West Chicago Avenue: Warehouse/offices, Willis J. McCauley, 1930

The long buff-painted warehouse building was one of the earliest and largest reinforced concrete buildings of its time. Designed by the Prairie School architect Hugh Garden, it has geometric, decorative motifs cast in the concrete and a strong horizontal emphasis, complementing the river. The spandrels, which were originally left unpainted, would have provided an even greater focus on horizontality. The original part of the structure was approximately 200 by 800 feet, but as space was needed, additional units were built.

The 619 Chicago Avenue building, to the south, bears some resemblance to the earlier structure, but its emphasis is more vertical, in keeping with the art deco style of the time. Atop this structure is a bronze figure of *Diana*, a version of P*rogress Lighting the Way for Commerce*, surmounted on Ward's Tower Building on Michigan Avenue.

N94
MONTGOMERY WARD CORPORATE OFFICES
535 West Chicago Avenue
Minoru Yamasaki & Associates, 1974

Yamasaki's simple tower, sheathed in travertine and glass, is a vertical contrast to the older Montgomery Ward buildings.

RIVER COTTAGES

MONTGOMERY WARD WAREHOUSE BUILDINGS

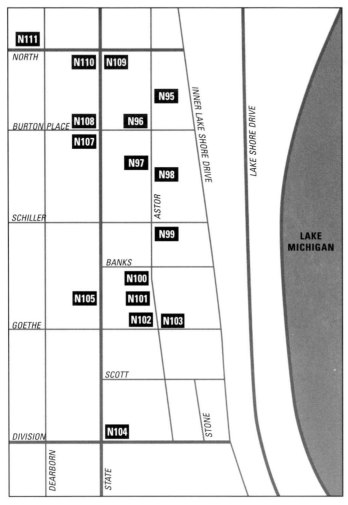

N95
1500 BLOCK OF ASTOR

N96
ROBERT W. PATTERSON
RESIDENCE
20 East Burton Place

N97
EDWARD P. RUSSELL
RESIDENCE
1444 North Astor

N98
H.N. MAY RESIDENCE
1443 North Astor

N99
JAMES CHARNLEY RESIDENCE
1365 North Astor

N100
POTTER PALMER
ROWHOUSES
*1316-1322 North Astor
and 25 East Banks*

N101
JAMES HOUGHTELING
ROWHOUSES
1308-1312 North Astor

N102
ASTOR TOWER
1300 North Astor

N103
1301 NORTH ASTOR

N104
FRANK FISHER APARTMENTS
1209 North State Parkway

N105
DOUBLE STUDIO FOR REBORI
AND SON
1328 North State Parkway

N106
GEORGE S. ISHAM RESIDENCE
1340 North State Parkway

N107
JOHN A. LYNCH
RESIDENCE
3 West Burton Place

N108
ALBERT F. MADLENER
RESIDENCE
4 West Burton Place

N109
ARCHBISHOP'S RESIDENCE
1555 North State Parkway

N110
1550 NORTH STATE PARKWAY

N111
CHICAGO HISTORICAL SOCIETY
Clark at North Avenue

THE GOLD COAST

The Gold Coast is an elegant residential area bordering the lake between Bellevue and North Avenues, where Chicago's wealthiest citizens lived near the end of the last century. Much of the original development of the Gold Coast was due to Potter Palmer, who built a castellated Gothic mansion at Lake Shore Drive and Banks in 1882. Alas, his and many other mansions along the drive are gone, for the economics of maintaining single family residences on such potentially high income properties is prohibitive.

Astor Street from North Avenue to Division and State Parkway from Division to North Avenue

NORTH

ROBERT W. PATTERSON RESIDENCE

EDWARD P. RUSSELL RESIDENCE

N95
1500 BLOCK OF ASTOR

Along this block are elegant and restrained townhouses, built primarily in the first decade of this century. The continuity of the street is the result of its consistent Georgian revival style and tasteful landscaping. A contrasting exception is the contemporary style house at 1524, designed by I.W. Coburn in 1968 to blend superbly with the existing adjacent structures.

N96
ROBERT W. PATTERSON RESIDENCE

20 East Burton Place
McKim, Mead & White, 1892; Remodeling and Addition; David Adler, 1927

Mayor Joseph Medill commissioned Stanford White to design this 5-story house, which he gave to his daughter and her husband as a wedding present. Inspired by a Renaissance palace, this mansion has strong symmetry, horizontal stringcourses articulating the three levels, and a balustrade hiding the roof. Upon a high brownstone base, the walls are a warm orange Roman brick with terra cotta, accented on the front by pink marble Doric and Ionic columns. Cyrus Hall McCormick II later purchased the house and commissioned David Adler to enlarge and remodel it in 1927. The residence was converted in 1980 to condominiums.

N97
EDWARD P. RUSSELL RESIDENCE

1444 North Astor
Holabird & Root, 1929

A superb example of the Art Deco style is this vertical 4-story townhouse, designed by the architects of the Board of Trade. The sophisticated facade is faced with smooth white limestone imported from France and trimmed in polished black granite. The profiles of the doors, the windows, and the shallow projecting iron bay provide subtle curves, which contrast with the otherwise stark design.

N98
H.N. MAY RESIDENCE

1443 North Astor
Joseph Lyman Silsbee, 1891

The Romanesque Revival house of rusticated granite was designed for the May family by Silsbee, who is known primarily for his role as an early employer of Frank Lloyd Wright and George W. Maher. In 1891, Wright was working for Sullivan, but Maher, still with Silsbee, may have worked on this unconventional house.

N99
JAMES CHARNLEY RESIDENCE

1365 North Astor
Adler & Sullivan, 1892

Designed by Frank Lloyd Wright working in the office of Adler & Sullivan, the Charnley house was one of the most modern structures in the world when built. It marks a drastic departure in residential architecture. Except for the delicate Sullivanesque colonnaded balcony and the patterns on the copper cornice, the house is stark in its broad geometric form. The facade is strongly horizontal, in contrast to the vertical townhouses around it, and heralds the Prairie houses of the 20th century. Wright's planning is highly evident on the interior, where the eleven rooms are arranged in an open plan around a central skylighted court with stairwell.

N100
POTTER PALMER ROWHOUSES

1316-1326 North Astor and 25 East Banks
Charles M. Palmer, 1889

Potter Palmer invested in dozens of houses for rental or resale in the Gold Coast. The five Romanesque revival houses in this group are especially distinctive, representing the best work of Charles Palmer (no relation to Potter Palmer). The units have tremendous variety of textures, colors and surface patterns, yet are visually tied together by repetitious shapes and continuous stringcourses.

N101
JAMES HOUGHTELING ROWHOUSES

1308-1312 North Astor
Burnham & Root, 1887

John Root designed four houses for Houghteling in the picturesque Queen Anne style. Of the three extant, Root lived in the center one at 1310, until his early death in 1891. His sister-in-law, Harriet Monroe, who founded *Poetry Magazine*, lived here until her death in 1936. Typical of the Queen Anne style are the grouped casement windows; the variety of materials including patterned terra cotta panels; and the steep chimneys and roofs, bays and turrets.

N102
ASTOR TOWER

1300 North Astor
Bertrand Goldberg, 1963

Originally a hotel with Maxim's Restaurant in the basement, this 28-story tower is now apartments. The reinforced concrete structure, supported on slender columns, was one of the first skyscrapers to invade the historic area.

POTTER PALMER ROWHOUSES

JAMES HOUGHTELING ROWHOUSES

ALBERT F. MADLENER RESIDENCE

N103
1301 NORTH ASTOR
Philip B. Maher, 1928

This elegant, Art Deco apartment building and one diagonally across the intersection of Astor and Goethe were built by Philip Maher, the son of the architect George Maher. The second generation Potter Palmers moved into the top three stories of this structure, encouraging the new fashion of apartment living. Compare the apartment building at 1260 Astor, built by the same architect two years later.

N104
FRANK FISHER APARTMENTS
1209 North State Parkway
Andrew Rebori, 1938

Rounded corners, painted white brick, and glass blocks are typical of the Art Deco style, of which this is an excellent example. Rebori collaborated with Chicago artist Edgar Miller, who designed the terra cotta plaques on the front.

N105
DOUBLE STUDIO FOR REBORI AND SON
1328 North State Parkway
Andrew N. Rebori, c. 1937; Remodeling: Bertrand Goldberg, 1956

Two separate studios, one facing the street and the other adjacent to the alley, were designed with a small courtyard between. The facade is much like the house by Rebori at 1209 North State Parkway. The wood panels on the facade were designed by artist Edgar Miller. In 1956, Bertrand Goldberg remodeled the studio for his mother-in-law, sculptress Lillian Florsheim. He added a bridge, including a kitchen, connecting the two studios.

N106
GEORGE S. ISHAM RESIDENCE
1340 North State Parkway
James Gamble Rogers, 1899

Built for a prominent surgeon, the Georgian style Isham house was more recently known as the Playboy Mansion after it was purchased in the 1960s by magazine publisher Hugh Hefner. In recent years the house served as a dormitory for the Art Institute of Chicago, but today it has returned to private hands.

N107
JOHN A. LYNCH RESIDENCE
3 West Burton Place
Jenney & Mundie, 1884

Designed by Jenney at the same time that he was working on his famous early skyscraper, the Home Insurance Building, this residence in the elegant French Renaissance style was seen as appropriate for a wealthy Chicago banker.

N108
ALBERT F. MADLENER RESIDENCE
4 West Burton Place
Richard E. Schmidt, 1902

Hugh Garden, working for Schmidt, designed this progressive Prairie School house. The geometry of the house's blocky mass, which is clad in brick and limestone, is emphasized by rectangular window groupings and horizontal stringcourses. Its unique ornament, concentrated around the doorway, is based on organic and geometric forms, and shows the influence of both Louis Sullivan and Frank Lloyd Wright. Built for a Chicago brewer, the house was occupied by the Madlener family until 1962, after which it was remodeled for use as headquarters of the Graham Foundation for Advanced Studies in the Fine Arts.

ARCHBISHOP'S RESIDENCE

CHICAGO HISTORICAL SOCIETY

N109
ARCHBISHOP'S RESIDENCE
1555 North State Parkway
Alfred F. Pashley, 1880

The Archbishop's mansion, one of the oldest structures in the area, is sited on spacious grounds, overlooking Lincoln Park. Typical of the English Queen Anne revival style, it is built of red pressed brick with corbelled bays and limestone trim. Its complicated silhouette includes steep gables, an octagonal tower, dormers, nineteen tall chimneys, and a *porte-cochere.*

N110
1550 NORTH STATE PARKWAY
Marshall & Fox, 1912

Benjamin Marshall designed and owned this apartment building, which was probably the most luxurious in Chicago when built. The French Baroque revival style, although elegant and beautiful, is pretentious; it therefore seems appropriate for the super-rich, who were leaving their single-family homes on Prairie Avenue and South Michigan Avenue to try apartment living on the North Side. The structure, clad in white glazed terra cotta, originally had one fifteen-room apartment per floor, with 7 spacious, high-ceilinged living rooms facing Lincoln Park and bedrooms facing the lake.

N111
CHICAGO HISTORICAL SOCIETY
Clark at North Avenue
Graham, Anderson, Probst & White, 1931; Alfred Shaw & Associates, 1972; Holabird & Root, 1988

Much of the original Georgian red brick building can still be seen on the east side facing Lincoln Park. As the historical society's collections grew, additional space was needed, and a large marble-faced wing was added to the west by Alfred Shaw in 1972. In 1988, Holabird & Root completed a larger addition encapsulating Shaw's addition in a wrapped-around structure sheathed with red brick and limestone to harmonize with the original building. Gerald Horn, designer for this last addition, conceived an entryway of steel trusses reflecting a classical pediment, from which hangs a grid of steel bars and hangers to which banners and current show announcements can be displayed.

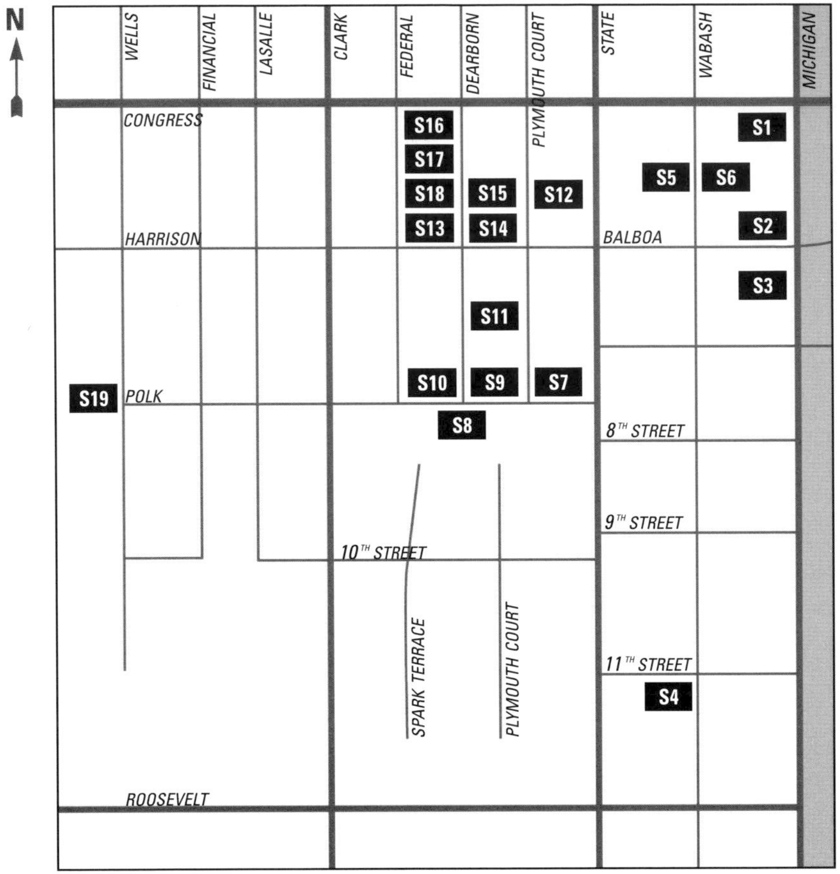

N
WELLS
FINANCIAL
LASALLE
CLARK
FEDERAL
DEARBORN
PLYMOUTH COURT
STATE
WABASH
MICHIGAN
CONGRESS
HARRISON
BALBOA
POLK
8TH STREET
9TH STREET
10TH STREET
11TH STREET
ROOSEVELT
SPARK TERRACE
PLYMOUTH COURT
S1
S2
S3
S4
S5
S6
S7
S8
S9
S10
S11
S12
S13
S14
S15
S16
S17
S18
S19

S1
CONGRESS HOTEL
504 South Michigan

S2
BLACKSTONE HOTEL AND THEATER
636 South Michigan

S3
CHICAGO HILTON AND TOWERS
720 South Michigan

S4
LUDINGTON BUILDING
1104 South Wabash

S5
WIRT DEXTER BUILDING
630 South Wabash

S6
COLUMBIA COLLEGE—WABASH CENTER
623 South Wabash

S7
COLUMBIA COLLEGE RESIDENCE CENTER
731 South Plymouth Court

S8
DEARBORN STATION
47 West Polk

S9
DONAHUE BUILDING AND ANNEX
701-21 South Dearborn

S10
SECOND FRANKLIN BUILDING
720 South Dearborn

S11
GRACE PLACE
637 South Dearborn

S12
MERGENTHALER BUILDING
531 South Plymouth Court

S13
PONTIAC BUILDING
522 South Dearborn

S14
TERMINALS BUILDING
537 South Dearborn

S15
OLD FRANKLIN BUILDING
525 South Dearborn

S16
HYATT ON PRINTERS' ROW
500 South Dearborn

S17
DUPLICATOR BUILDING
530 South Dearborn

S18
MORTON BUILDING
538 South Dearborn

S19
RIVER CITY
800 South Wells

SOUTH LOOP

The district immediately south of the central Loop includes a hotel district along South Michigan and a warehouse and light manufacturing area to the west. Especially interesting is Printers' Row on South Dearborn and Plymouth Court, between Congress and Polk. Printer's Row is dominated by turn-of-the-century printing houses, designed for large spaces, abundant light, and floors which would support heavy printing presses and the storage of books. Several architects and developers around 1975 began efforts to renovate the area. Harry Weese, Larry Booth and several others formed the South Dearborn Renovations Associates Ltd, since renamed the Community Resources Corp. Taking advantage of federal investment tax credits available through the Tax Reform Act, buildings were purchased, the zoning was changed, and loft space was converted to residential units. Today the area represents a success story in transformation, a unique blend of businesses, offices, apartments, condominiums, and restaurants.

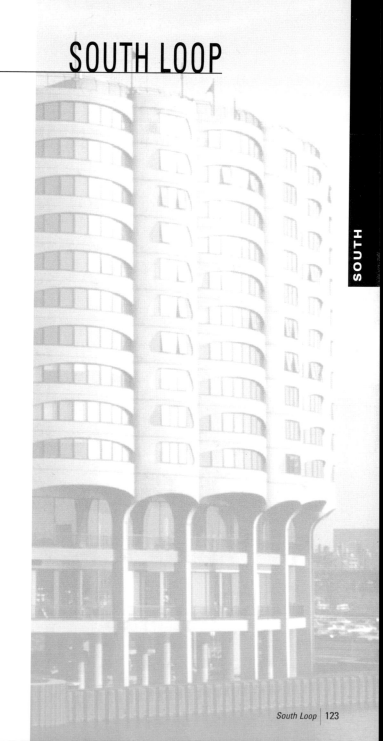

SOUTH

BLACKSTONE HOTEL AND THEATER

LUDINTON BUILDING

S1
CONGRESS HOTEL
504 South Michigan
Clinton J. Warren, 1893; Holabird & Roche, 1902, 1907

Called originally the Auditorium Annex, this structure was built just four years after the Auditorium Building. Its Romanesque revival design was a deliberate attempt to relate its window patterns and comparable roofline to the earlier building. The south addition at 520, by Holabird & Roche, is four stories taller. In the lobby of the original hotel, mosaics and art-and-crafts motifs are somewhat reminiscent of Sullivan's work.

S2
BLACKSTONE HOTEL AND THEATER
636 South Michigan
Marshall & Fox, 1909, 1911

One of Chicago's tallest buildings in 1909, this 22-story hotel is French in design, relating to some of the Baroque revival creations of Paris during the Second Empire. Rising above a pink granite base with high arched openings is a shaft of red brick trimmed with white terra cotta. An elegant and very steep and rounded mansard roof crowns the whole, looking rather out of character in Chicago. The five-story theater, built two years later, is the structure to the west.

S3
CHICAGO HILTON AND TOWERS
720 South Michigan
Holabird & Roche, 1927

Once the "world's largest hotel", the Hilton had nearly 3000 rooms. After a $150 million renovation in the 1980s, its room count was reduced to about 1600. This blocky structure, broken into projecting wings, combines a limestone base, a brick shaft and a limestone summit. The top stories and towers, with their Ionic columns and balustrades, relate to the restrained Baroque style of the *Grand* and *Petit Trianon* structures at Versailles. The opulent lobby, just inside the entrance on Michigan Avenue, is a towering space, rich in ornamentation, with a grand baroque staircase and a ceiling painted with clouds against a blue sky.

S4
LUDINGTON BUILDING
1104 South Wabash
Jenney & Mundie, 1891

One of William LeBaron Jenney's best designs, the Ludington is a steel skeleton frame clad in white terra cotta. Although the classical pilasters and moldings are ornate, the ornament is subordinate to the grid-like structure.

S5
WIRT DEXTER BUILDING
630 South Wabash Avenue
Adler & Sullivan, 1887

The Wirt Dexter Building is important as one of the few Adler & Sullivan structures remaining in the city. As with many of their smaller works, the building's facade has a wide central bay, flanked by narrower ones on either side. Because of its warehouse function, its ornament is minimal, existing only of two slender Egyptoid mullions rising from the second to the fifth stories.

S6
COLUMBIA COLLEGE—WABASH CENTER
(Second Studebaker Building)
623 South Wabash Avenue
Solon S. Beman, 1896

The Studebaker Carriage Company left their previous home on Michigan Avenue, also designed by Beman and now known as the Fine Arts Building, to move into this large, glassy ten-story skyscraper. One must look above the remodeling of the first three stories to appreciate the original structure. Although Beman incorporated a great deal of Gothic detail, including an elaborate cornice, which is missing, his design clearly reflects the building's slender steel skeleton.

COLUMBIA COLLEGE RESIDENCE CENTER

S7
COLUMBIA COLLEGE RESIDENCE CENTER
(Formerly Lakeside Press Building)
731 South Plymouth Court
Howard van Doren Shaw; Samuel A. Treat, Associate, 1897, 1902; Adaptive reuse: Lisec & Biederman

Mannerist, decorative and certainly creative is this printing house built for R.R. Donnelley. The eclectic building has everything: arches, colonnettes, quoins, carved lions, and medallions. Note the Indian chief in the Donnelley seal. The building's structure, however, is clear, with projecting piers alternating with recessed spandrel panels, mullions and window frames.   The building has been converted to student housing.

S8
DEARBORN STATION
47 West Polk
Cyrus C.L. Eidlitz, 1885; Adaptive reuse: Hasbrouck-Hunderman, 1983

The only surviving 19th century railroad station in Chicago, the structure is the architectural gem and serves as the visual focus of South Dearborn Street. Its eclectic front combines Romanesque and Italianate details with a somewhat Renaissance tower. Today it looks more Italianate because of the absence of its steep roof covering the whole and an even steeper Swiss German-style roof surmounting the tower. Horizontality is emphasized by a pink granite base, by courses of dark brick, which alternate periodically with red pressed brick in the walls above, and by the crisp ornate terra cotta patterns of the cornice. Much of the terra cotta and the iron staircase railings are examples of the Aesthetic Movement, somewhat related to designs by Louis Sullivan or Frank Furness around 1880. Today the station is a shopping and office facility. The San Francisco firm Kaplan/McLaughlin/Diaz designed the large addition to the south of the station where the train shed once stood.

S9
DONAHUE BUILDING AND ANNEX
701-21 South Dearborn
Julius Speyer, 1883; Annex: Alfred Alschuler, 1913; Adaptive reuse: Harry Weese & Associates, 1983

The Romanesque-style Donahue Building has large polished granite columns with acanthus capitals and a rusticated brownstone arch at its entrance. It was originally owned by Donahue and Henneberrg, a company which operated forty printing presses in the basement. Small publishing companies, which utilized the printing facilities, rented space in the building. The books were bound on the seventh and eighth floors. The ten-story annex, while blending with the original, is more functional in design.

DEARBORN STATION

SECOND FRANKLIN BUILDING

MERGENTHALER BUILDING

S10
SECOND FRANKLIN BUILDING
720 South Dearborn
George C. Nimmons, 1912; Adaptive reuse: Lisec & Biederman, 1987

One of the most beautiful and certainly the most colorful buildings on the street is this 13-story brown brick printing house, whose presses continued their operation until 1983. The building reflects its structure with bold projecting piers from the second to the ninth floors. Colored enameled bricks create patterns, with the brown brick giving a tapestry effect and suggesting pilasters. On the ground level, nine tapering pilasters with pentagon-shaped capitals separate the store windows. Foremost, however, are Viennese artist Oskar Gross' glazed ceramic mosaic murals on the spandrels depicting the invention of the printing press and other episodes from the history of printing. The building has been converted to condominiums.

S11
GRACE PLACE
637 South Dearborn
Anonymous Architect, 1915; Adaptive reuse: Booth/Hansen & Associates, 1985

This 3-story warehouse building, sensitively converted into a non-conventional Episcopal church, provides an interesting combination of materials, textures, and shapes: exposed brickwork and heavy rough-hewn timber framing, gray-painted ductwork, porthole windows, and in the sanctuary a dramatic circular wall and a metal cross.

S12
MERGENTHALER BUILDING
531 South Plymouth Court
Anonymous Architect, 1886; Remodeling: Schmidt, Garden and Martin, 1917

The window groupings in this printing warehouse, which has been now converted to condominiums, were progressive for 1886. The second through fifth stories are grouped under wide arches at the fifth story. The sixth story windows are smaller and create a horizontal visual rhythm. The facade at sidewalk level, which has some Prairie characteristics, is from the 1917 remodeling by Schmidt, Garden and Martin .

S13
PONTIAC BUILDING
542 South Dearborn
Holabird & Roche, 1891; Adaptive reuse: Booth/Hansen & Associates, 1985

The oldest Holabird & Roche building remaining in downtown Chicago, the 14-story Pontiac is less reflective of its steel skeleton than most of the firm's buildings of the period. The exterior is sheathed with dark brick and red terra cotta trim. Very wide projecting bays flank a central bay and extend for most of the building's height.

S14
TERMINALS BUILDING
(Ellsworth Building)
537 South Dearborn
John M. Van Osdel & Company, 1892; Adaptive reuse: Community Resources Corporation, 1986

This 15-story building, which has a steel frame faced with rusticated limestone as base and vertical brick piers above, was probably the product of John Mills Van Osdel II, who directed the company after the death of his father in 1891.

S15
OLD FRANKLIN BUILDING
525 South Dearborn
Bauman & Lotz, 1887; Adaptive reuse: Booth/Hansen & Associates, 1983

One of the oldest structures on the block is this warehouse, which demonstrates en early development toward what later became known as Chicago commercial style: brick piers, terra cotta capitals, windows which practically fill the bays, recessed spandrels, and arched openings at the top. Note the exposed turnbuckles. The building now has 54 apartments above the commercial ground floor.

S16
HYATT ON PRINTERS' ROW
500 South Dearborn
Adaptive Reuse and Addition: Booth/Hanson & Associates, 1986

While keeping the facades of the Duplicator and Morton Buildings intact, Booth/Hanson added a modern corner structure with strong affinity with Chicago's turn-of-the-century heritage. The new addition has the same height and spandrel levels as the Duplicator Building.

S17
DUPLICATOR BUILDING
530 South Dearborn
Edward P. Baumann, 1886

Although now part of the Hyatt Hotel, the visual integrity of the original structure is kept. This former warehouse is a more straightforward design than Baumann's Old Franklin across the street. The facade has three unequal bays separated by wide brick piers. The two wider bays on the south are split by brick mullions, which are narrower versions of the piers.

S18
MORTON BUILDING
538 South Dearborn
Jenney & Mundie, 1896

The 12-story Morton Building, a steel skeleton sheathed with yellow brick and terra cotta, is one of Jenney's more decorative designs, probably influenced by the Columbian exposition. Its classical details include egg-and-dart moldings, dentils, lion's heads, Renaissance flowers, plume borders, and even caryatids, which seem to support the projecting bays.

RIVER CITY

S19
RIVER CITY
800 South Wells
Bertrand Goldberg Associates, 1986

The molded curvilinear forms of this reinforced concrete structure at the river's edge are related in form to Goldberg's earlier work at Marina City and at the Hilliard Center. Here apartments face an interior winding street, which brings continuity to two interlocking serpentine-shaped buildings. A variety of businesses and services are provided in the lower levels. Goldberg conceived this as the first of several phases of a monumental construction project, which would ultimately cover the river area between Congress and Roosevelt.

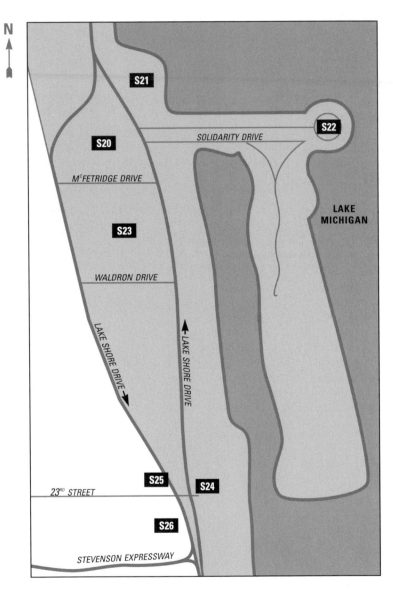

N

S21

S20

S22

SOLIDARITY DRIVE

M^cFETRIDGE DRIVE

S23

WALDRON DRIVE

LAKE
MICHIGAN

LAKE SHORE DRIVE

LAKE SHORE DRIVE

S25

S24

23RD STREET

S26

STEVENSON EXPRESSWAY

S20
FIELD MUSEUM OF
NATURAL HISTORY
*Roosevelt Road and South
Lake Shore Drive*

S21
JOHN G. SHEDD AQUARIUM
1200 South Lake Shore Drive

S22
ADLER PLANETARIUM
900 East Achsah Bond Drive

S23
SOLDIER FIELD
425 East McFetridge Drive

S24
M^cCORMICK PLACE EAST
2301 South Lake Shore Drive

S25
M^cCORMICK PLACE NORTH
450 East 23rd Street

S26
M^cCORMICK PLACE SOUTH
*2301 South Martin Luther King
Drive*

SOUTH LAKE SHORE DRIVE

The development of the lakefront south of Grant Park for public enjoyment and recreation was a modified execution of the Chicago Plan of 1909. Burnham himself designed the Field Museum, although it was not completed until eight years after his death in 1912. The Plan also called for a stadium and planetarium, although these, too, were not built until some years later.

JOHN G. SHEDD AQUARIUM

JOHN G. SHEDD OCEANARIUM

S20
FIELD MUSEUM OF NATURAL HISTORY
Roosevelt Road and South Lake Shore Drive
D.H. Burnham & Company, 1906-1912; Burnham, Graham & Company, 1912-17; Graham, Anderson, Probst & White, 1917-20

The Field Museum, like many of the museums of the world, is severe and classical. Its style was probably influenced by Charles Atwood's design for the Fine Arts Building of the World's Columbian Exposition, today the Museum of Science and Industry. The Field Museum is of white Georgia marble, complete with colonnaded walls and porticos, caryatids, pediments and antefixes. The central hall, 76 feet high, is entered at either end through an immense, projecting temple front. Smaller porticos project forward at the end of each wing of the building. The interior of the central hall is one of Chicago's finest neo-classical spaces.

S21
JOHN G. SHEDD AQUARIUM
1200 South Lake Shore Drive
Graham, Anderson, Probst & White, 1929; Oceanarium, Lohan Associates, 1991

A Greek, Doric-style front, blending with the classical Field Museum across the street, provides an impressive entrance for the octagonal aquarium of white Georgia marble. The structure is covered with a variety of aquatic motifs and crowned with a pyramidal roof and skylight. Lohan's Oceanarium addition manages to join a semicircular structure of a very different style, yet without marring the integrity of the earlier building. The new structure surrounds a 3-million gallon tank, holding whales, dolphins, sea otters and seals, with a 50-foot high glass curtain wall. The ingenious design gives visitors seeing Lake Michigan in the background the illusion that interior and exterior merge.

S22
ADLER PLANETARIUM
900 East Achsah Bond Drive

Ernest A. Grunsfeld, 1930; Subterranean addition: C.F. Murphy Associates, 1975; Entrance addition: Lohan Associates, 1991

The twelve sides of this structure of pink variegated rainbow granite rise in concentric tiers. Utilizing Art Deco geometry, the building is pristine in its simplicity. The twelve sides represent the zodiac, as do the twelve bronze plaques at the corners by Alfonso Iannelli. The domed roof, covered with green copper, supports an interior domed ceiling on which the stars are projected. This was the first public planetarium in America, built just in time for the Century of Progress world's fair at the site.

S23
SOLDIER FIELD
425 East McFetridge Drive
Holabird & Roche, 1922-24

In 1919 Holabird & Roche won a competition for the design of this structure, originally called Grant Park Stadium. At its dedication ceremony in 1925, Governor Frank Lowden said, "Let it be a memorial to all the fallen heroes of all the wars ever fought." The design could be that of a mausoleum, but for its Cyclopean proportions. On its east and west sides, majestic colonnades of paired 100-foot high cast concrete Doric columns rise above the stadium. Designed to recall ancient classical games, the forms also harmonize with the earlier classical structures in Burnham Park.

S24
McCORMICK PLACE EAST
2301 South Lake Shore Drive
C.F. Murphy Associates, 1971

Gene Summers, designer for C.F. Murphy, received his Masters of Architecture degree under Mies van der Rohe at Illinois Institute of Technology in 1951 and worked in Mies's office from 1950 to 1966. Built on the foundation of a previous convention center, which had burned in 1967, the structure might be thought of as two buildings, each with glazed, fifty-foot high walls, under one immense roof. One unit holds the Arie Crown Theater, while the other unit is a vast convention and exhibition hall with a 300,000 square-foot surface, interrupted by only eight columns. The roof is a space-frame, or 3-way truss, 15 feet deep, 750 feet wide and 1350 feet long (19 acres), carried by 36 reinforced concrete supports and cantilevered 75 feet on all sides.

S25
McCORMICK PLACE NORTH
450 East 23rd Street
Skidmore, Owings, & Merrill, 1986

Heading the design team was Diane Legge, the first woman to become a partner in the S.O.M. firm. The most striking aspect of the design is its roof, a 15-foot deep space-frame supported by steel cables hung from twelve concrete pylons. Fixed vertical pipes on the long sides carry the cables downward where they are buttressed in the ground. In Legge's design of the facades, triangular gray aluminum panels form a frieze, which relate visually to the negative triangular shapes between the cables and the pylons. The diagonal patterns on the walls were also Legge's attempt to pay homage to an unbuilt Mies van der Rohe exhibition hall design. Coincidentally, Ms. Legge was at the time married to Dirk Lohan, grandson of Mies van der Rohe. Circular domed pavilions on the bridge connecting with the East Building are delightful in themselves, but incongruous with the two exhibition halls.

S26
McCORMICK PLACE SOUTH
2301 South Martin Luther King Drive
Thompson Ventulett Stainback & Associates;
A.Epstein & Sons International, Associate
Architects, 1997

The design of McCormick Place South is very different from McCormick East or North. It is less sophisticated, lacking the clarity and unity of the two earlier structures. On the other hand, from the functional point of view, it works well. Its sweeping galleria links the three McCormick structures together and links the city with the lakefront.

MCCORMICK PLACE NORTH

MCCORMICK PLACE SOUTH

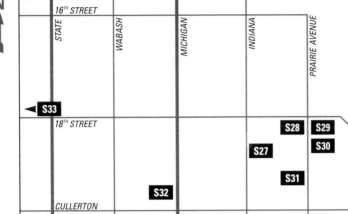

S27
HENRY B. CLARKE
RESIDENCE
1855 South Indiana

S28
JOHN JACOB GLESSNER
RESIDENCE
1800 Prairie Avenue

S29
WILLIAM W. KIMBALL
RESIDENCE
1801 Prairie Avenue

S30
JOSEPH G. COLEMAN
RESIDENCE
1811 Prairie Avenue

S31
ELBRIDGE KEITH
RESIDENCE
1900 Prairie Avenue

S32
SECOND PRESBYTERIAN
CHURCH
1936 South Michigan

S33
SCHOENHOFEN BREWERY
1800 South Canalport

S34
RAYMOND HILLIARD
CENTER
2030 South State

PRAIRIE AVENUE AND VICINITY

Prairie Avenue began to be populated in the 1860s, but its heyday began in the 1870s when several blocks between 16th and 22nd Streets became extremely fashionable. Many of the wealthy residents who had lived on the periphery of the central Loop began moving south, perhaps in part to remove themselves from the danger of another great fire or to distance themselves from other undesirable features of the city. In 1876 Marshall Field hired society architect Richard M. Hunt to design his house in the 1900 block, purported to have cost $2,000,000. Shortly afterward George Pullman, designer of sleeping and dining railway cars, arranged for Solon S. Beman to build his mansion at the northeast corner of Prairie and Eighteenth. The price of real estate on the street soared.

Today one sees the results of dramatic social and economic transformation of the neighborhood, a process which has been going on for over a hundred years. Even as early as the 1880s, some of the wealthy residents began to move away from Prairie Avenue to the Gold Coast, following Potter Palmer's development of that area. By 1906 factories began to invade the street, and from that time, deterioration of the residential stock accelerated. Preservation-minded citizens and architectural organizations, after years of effort to save what remains of value, have established the Prairie Avenue Historic District and preserved some of the existing homes. Glessner House and the Henry B. Clarke House are open to the public. In the small park between these two structures is a sculpture by Carl Rohl-Smith commemorating the Massacre of 1812, in which a hostile band of Potawatomi Indians ambushed a group of settlers attempting to flee from Fort Dearborn. A plaque near the corner of 18th Street and Prairie Avenue marks the supposed site.

HENRY BL CLARKE HOUSE

JOHN JACOB GLESSNER HOUSE

S27
HENRY B. CLARKE RESIDENCE
1855 South Indiana
John C. Rue, builder, 1836

At a time when most buildings in Chicago were log cabins or of the newly invented "balloon" construction, Henry Clarke hired the carpenter John C. Rue to construct for him this much more substantial Greek Revival house. Rue might just as well have called himself an architect, since architectural education in America at the time was non-existent. Only one year after the construction of the Chicago City Hall and Courthouse in the Greek Revival, the style immediately became popular. The Clarke house is almost a stereotype of the style. It is built high off the ground with a flight of steps leading to a four-columned portico, crowned with an entablature and pediment in the fashion of a classical temple (actually more Roman than Greek). It is completely symmetrical with a center door, two identical tall triple-sash windows flanking each side of the entrance, a frieze of low "belly-flop" windows above. The plan has a central hall with two primary rooms on either side. The interiors of the house have been furnished by the Colonial Dames of Illinois in keeping with the styles typical of the 1840s.

The house was built originally on a 20-acre farm near 16th Street and Michigan Avenue. After Henry Clarke died in a cholera epidemic in 1849, the "Widow" Clarke began selling off lots, to make improvements to the house and support her children. At this time, she had a cupola built in the Italianate style. The house has moved twice: her children sold it in 1872 to owners who had it moved to 4526 South Wabash. In 1977, having become seriously dilapidated, it was purchased by the city of Chicago and moved to its present location. The move was a spectacular feat, involving lifting the 120-ton structure above the elevated railway structure.

S28
JOHN JACOB GLESSNER RESIDENCE
1800 Prairie Avenue
Henry Hobson Richardson, 1885-87

Although designed in a version of the popular Romanesque revival style, the Glessner house was, at the same time, one of the most modern houses in the world. Its horizontality and simplicity were radical, "honest", and unpretentious. Surrounded when built by ornate, stylish houses of huge dimensions, this restrained horizontal fortress-like structure set close to the street made quite a contrast, and neighbors were quick to ridicule it. Contributing to its horizontal look were the low entrance, one step off the ground, and its low, wide front door under an arch of long, narrow voussoirs, as well as its horizontal bands of second story windows, all characteristics which would later become part of Frank Lloyd Wright's style.

The Glessners' architect, H.H. Richardson of Boston, was famous for his massive Romanesque style. Windows are deeply recessed into thick, rusticated walls of pink granite, which provide insulation against the cold north winds and the clatter and whistles from the Illinois Central Railway a block to the east. Although the house is slightly asymmetrical because of the *porte-cochere* to the south, it stands dignified and orderly. The details are beautifully executed: the elegant proportions of the front door and its iron grill, the carved stone within the arch and the capitals of the colonnettes serving as mullions, the red mortar joints between the massive blocks of the wall.

Oriented toward an interior courtyard, major rooms have larger windows facing south and west. The courtyard, informal and protected from street noise, served as a private outdoor living area. The Chicago Architecture Foundation, owner of the structure, has restored the house and furnished most of the primary rooms in the Arts-and-Crafts style, much as it was in the Glessners' day. Chicago is indeed fortunate that this structure, which had been threatened with demolition in 1966, has been saved and preserved. It is one of Richardson's best and his only remaining work in our city.

S29
WILLIAM W. KIMBALL RESIDENCE
1801 Prairie Avenue
Solon S. Beman, 1892

Kimball chose Beman as his architect on the recommendation of George Pullman, whose house was just to the north. Beman had designed Pullman's house as well as the town of Pullman. The design for Kimball, a piano manufacturer, was French Renaissance, or "French Chateau," since it imitated the *Chateau de Josselin* in Brittany. The roof is particularly characteristic of this style, slightly more sloping than a mansard roof. The exterior walls, built of smooth gray Bedford limestone with rounded towers and bays, are trimmed with delicate Renaissance low relief ornament. The interior is paneled in oak and mahogany, and some of the fireplaces are onyx.

S30
JOSEPH G. COLEMAN RESIDENCE
1811 Prairie Avenue
Cobb & Frost, 1885

The rusticated brown sandstone walls, large entry arch and foliated colonnettes are typical of the Romanesque revival style. Along with Romanesque characteristics, however, the Coleman house exhibits a sensitive blending of a Queen Anne revival style: the steep roof, tall chimneys, dormer windows, and a rich mixture of various materials. The house was converted for office use in the 1920s.

S31
ELBRIDGE KEITH RESIDENCE
1900 Prairie Avenue
Anonymous Architect, 1870

Pretentious and grand, the large Keith house is the earliest extant home in the Prairie Avenue Historic District. Its Second Empire style, with mansard roof and dormers, was especially popular among the upper classes just before or after the Chicago fire. Except for the roof, the house could be called Italianate, with its ornate bracketed cornice and tall, narrow arched windows. Elbridge Keith and his brother owned a wholesale millinery business.

S32
SECOND PRESBYTERIAN CHURCH
1936 South Michigan
James Renwick, 1874; Rebuilding, Howard Van Doren Shaw, 1900

This English Gothic church, built of Lemont limestone ashlar with sandstone trim, has a cruciform plan with a square tower. It is in fact a rebuilding of an earlier church by James Renwick (1849), which burned. The degree of Renwick's involvement in the supervision of the original or the rebuilding is ambiguous. Even more significant, however, is the magnificent Arts-and-Crafts interior of the church, which dates from 1900. After a fire had destroyed the roof and resulted in water damage to the interior, Howard Van Doren Shaw undertook the reconstruction of roof and interior. Murals are by Frederick Clay Bartlett; eight of the stained glass windows are by the workshops of Tiffany, two by Burne-Jones, and others by the studios of William Morris, John LaFarge, and Healy & Millet.

S33
SCHOENHOFEN BREWERY
1800 South Canalport
Richard E. Schmidt, 1902

Hugh Garden was no doubt responsible for this unusual Prairie School building. The trapezoidal-shaped structure served as warehouse as well as power-house for the brewery. The facade is a play of horizontal and vertical linear brickwork patterns. This complex play of rectangles with brick banding is typical of Garden's work, as can be seen also in his designs for the Madlener House and the Chapin & Gore Building.

WILLIAM W. KIMBALL RESIDENCE

S34
RAYMOND HILLIARD CENTER
2030 South State
Bertrand Goldberg, 1966

The Chicago Housing Authority sponsored this low-income housing consisting of four towers. Two are 16-story and cylindrical, scalloped or flower-like in plan, with wedge-shaped apartments for the elderly and central cores for service facilities, similar in concept to the design of Marina City. The towers are connected by a one-story community center. Two additional, gently-curving towers with long arc-shaped plans are for younger families. Landscaping includes an outdoor theater and playground equipment.

N

DAN RYAN EXPRESSWAY
FEDERAL
STATE
WABASH
MICHIGAN
INDIANA
PRAIRIE AVENUE
CALUMET AVENUE

29TH STREET

31ST STREET

S38

32ND STREET

S35b | S35e | S36

S35a

S35f

S35i | S35d

33RD STREET

S35i | S35g | S37

S35c

35TH STREET

S35h

S35
ILLINOIS INSTITUTE OF
TECHNOLOGY
3100 to 3500 South State

S35a
ALUMNI MEMORIAL HALL
3201 South Dearborn

S35b
COMMONS BUILDING
3200 South Wabash

S35c
CROWN HALL
3360 South State

S35d
PERLSTEIN HALL
10 West 33rd Street

S35e
ST. SAVIOR CHAPEL
65 East 32nd Street

S35f
GROVER M. HERMANN HALL
3241 South Federal

S35g
PAUL V. GALVIN LIBRARY
35 West 33rd Street

S35h
RESEARCH INSTITUTE TOWER
3424 South State

S35i
ARMOUR INSTITUTE BUILDINGS
*3300 South Federal, 100 West 33rd
Street*

S36
ROLOSON HOUSES
3213-19 South Calumet

S37
PILGRIM BAPTIST CHURCH
3101 South Indiana

S18
SIDNEY A. KENT RESIDENCE
2944 South Michigan Boulevard

ILLINOIS INSTITUTE OF TECHNOLOGY AND VICINITY

South Michigan Avenue around 35th Street, sometimes called "Millionaire's Row," rivaled Prairie Avenue and the Gold Coast in the late 19th Century with some of the city's most expensive homes. In the early 20th Century, however, the area underwent a reverse transformation, becoming almost entirely slum. The construction of the Illinois Institute of Technology campus unfortunately required the destruction of many significant but dilapidated mansions. Today some of the nearby residential areas are undergoing a healthy gentrification.

SOUTH

CROWN HALL

S35
ILLINOIS INSTITUTE OF TECHNOLOGY
3100 to 3500 South State

The German architect Mies van der Rohe, former director of the famous German art and architecture school, the Bauhaus, was brought to Chicago in 1938 to head the Department of Architecture at Armour Institute of Technology. In 1940, after Armour Institute merged with Lewis Institute, the new school took the name Illinois Institute of Technology and hired Mies to design its new campus. Laid out on graph paper with floor plans and elevations based on a 24-foot module (although with certain variations on the module), the campus has a high degree of continuity and harmony. Mies also believed in the straightforward expression of structural form, which he articulated through the painting of structural members black and through deliberate exhibition of structural details. Nowhere in America is the rationalism of the International Style more prominent than here on the I.I.T. campus. Not only was Mies' philosophy made indelible in the physical environment, but his students went forth to propagate his theories. Some of his more outstanding students continued to be associated with I.I.T. as instructors and as architects of the later campus buildings.

S35a
ALUMNI MEMORIAL HALL
3201 South Dearborn
Mies van der Rohe, 1946

The steel structure, which had to be fireproofed, is hidden behind I-beams, which perform as mullions supporting the infill while at the same time visually representing the structure. Notice the reentrant corners designed to exhibit the skeleton structure and its I-beam mullion counterpart.

S35b
COMMONS BUILDING
3200 South Wabash
Ludwig Mies van der Rohe, 1953

The form of this pristine steel and glass box is somewhat incongruous with the multi-functional character of the building. Originally the student cafeteria was the structure's central purpose.

S35c
CROWN HALL
3360 South State
Ludwig Mies van der Rohe, 1956

In many ways, Crown Hall is the jewel of the campus. It is the most "classical" of all the university buildings with its horizontal dimensions, perfect symmetry, raised floor, and regularity. A single space of immense proportions, 120 by 220 feet with no interior supports, it was called by Mies, "Universal Space," meaning having complete flexibility. The roof covering this huge interior space is supported by four immense, rectangular "portal arches," each consisting of a steel girder welded on either end to an H-column. The entrances on the north and south walls are six feet off the ground, reached via elegant travertine steps and platforms.

S35d
PERLSTEIN HALL
10 West 33rd Street
Ludwig Mies van der Rohe, 1946

This was originally built as metallurgical and chemical engineering laboratories.

S35e
ST. SAVIOR CHAPEL
65 East 32nd Street
Ludwig Mies van der Rohe, 1952

Nothing from the exterior of this small structure proclaims itself to be a church. Its aesthetic is "universal" for it encloses space which could be adapted to any purpose. The visual focus of this stark nondenominational space is a solid travertine altar.

S35f
GROVER M. HERMANN HALL
3241 South Federal
Skidmore, Owings & Merrill, 1962

Designed by partner Walter Netsch, the structure functions as the student union, with cafeteria and various student facilities.

S35g
PAUL V. GALVIN LIBRARY
35 West 33rd Street
Skidmore, Owings & Merrill, 1962

Walter Netsch designed the university library along with Hermann Hall to its north. Neither building has the refinement and subtlety of Mies's designs. The library entrance is at the lower level, below grade.

PERLSTEIN HALL

AMOUR INSTITUTE

ROLOSON HOUSES

S35h
RESEARCH INSTITUTE TOWER
3424 South State
Schmidt, Garden & Erikson, 1965

S35i
ARMOUR INSTITUTE BUILDINGS
Main Building, *3300 South Federal,* Patton & Fisher, 1893
Machinery Hall, *100 West 33rd Street,* Patton, Fisher & Miller, 1901

These two picturesque Romanesque revival buildings combine rusticated stone with red pressed brick. The former tower of the Main Building burned in 1947 and was removed. The same structure has unusual large-scale dormers featuring Palladian-type windows. The Romanesque style was typical of Patton & Fisher, who specialized in the design of schools and libraries. William LeBaron Jenney taught in this former "manual training school", where many early Chicago architects studied.

S36
ROLOSON HOUSES
3213-19 South Calumet
Frank Lloyd Wright, 1894

The area called "The Gap," just east of I.I.T., is filled with late 19th century stone and brick houses. Although many are in a somewhat dilapidated state, there is much restoration in progress. Most notable are the "Tudor" style townhouses, which Wright designed very early in his career before he had formulated the Prairie style. Wright's "Victorian" period is one of his most interesting, for we see the evolution of his concepts relating to the geometric interacting of horizontal and vertical forms, Sullivanesque organic ornament, and open planning.

S37
PILGRIM BAPTIST CHURCH
(Originally *Kehilath Anshe Ma'ariv* Synagogue)
3301 South Indiana
Adler & Sullivan, 1891

Dankbar Adler's father was the rabbi of this congregation from 1861 to 1883, thus the commission to Adler & Sullivan. The highly unusual, and somewhat mannerist, proportions of the structure would suggest that perhaps Adler had more to do with the basic form than Sullivan. There is no question, however, of Sullivan's design of the profuse ornament on the interior. Ornate friezes enhance the arches behind the altar, encircle the hall at the base of its barrel-vaulted ceiling, and enliven the face of the balcony, which wraps three sides of the room. Sullivan worked with the decorating firm Healy & Millet, which carried out the russet-beige-gold color scheme for the ornament and the art glass windows.

S38
SIDNEY A. KENT RESIDENCE
2944 South Michigan Boulevard
Burnham & Root, 1882-3

The massing and delicate low relief ornament of this elegant dwelling could be called French Renaissance, although the combination of red brick and terra cotta, as well as the baroque gable, give it a Dutch feeling. Kent purchased the wrought iron fence at the Columbian Exposition of 1893. The house has been converted into five luxury apartments.

PILGRIM BAPTIST CHURCH

SIDNEY A. KENT RESIDENCE

W1
CHICAGO CENTRAL POST OFFICE
433 West Van Buren

W2
GATEWAY CENTER IV
300 South Riverside Plaza

W3
MID-AMERICA COMMODITY EXCHANGE
444 West Jackson

W4
UNION STATION
210 South Canal

W5
FLORSHEIM SHOE COMPANY
130 South Canal

W6
GATEWAY CENTER III
222 South Riverside Plaza

W7
GATEWAY CENTER I
10 South Riverside Plaza

W8
GATEWAY CENTER II
120 South Riverside Plaza

W9
525 WEST MADISON

W10
ILLINOIS BELL TELEPHONE BUILDING
10 South Canal

W11
525 WEST MONROE

W12
HELLER INTERNATIONAL TOWER
500 West Monroe

W13
RIVERSIDE PLAZA
2 North Riverside Plaza / 400 West Madison

W14
CITICORP CENTER
500 West Madison

W15
MORTON INTERNATIONAL BUILDING
100 North Canal

W16
RIVER CENTER
111 North Canal

W17
RANDOLPH PLACE
165 North Canal

W18
PRESIDENTIAL TOWERS
555, 575, 605, 625 West Madison

W19
HAROLD WASHINGTON SOCIAL SECURITY ADMINISTRATION BUILDING
600 West Madison

W20
IIT-KENT COLLEGE OF LAW
565 West Adams

W21
ST. PATRICK'S CHURCH
140 South Desplaines

GATEWAY DISTRICT

From Jackson and Canal, North on Canal,
West on Randolph, South on Clinton, West on Adams

The district just west of the Chicago River is called Gateway. For many visitors and commuters to Chicago, this is the entrance to the Loop. The city's primary rail stations—Union Station and Northwestern Station—are here. Renovation of this district has ,been going on for almost thirty years beginning with the construction of the AT&T Building on Canal and Gateway I and II. But the massive change in population came with the building of Presidential Towers, which enticed thousands of "yuppies" into the old "Skid Row," thus displacing the slums with safer, though fortress-like, housing.

GATEWAY CENTER IV

MID-AMERICA COMMODITY EXCHANGE

W1
CHICAGO CENTRAL POST OFFICE
433 West Van Buren
Graham Anderson Probst and White, 1929

Typical of the Art Deco style, which was adopted by many post offices throughout the country, the massing is blocky and detailing is geometric. Chicago's post office is unique in spanning the Congress Expressway. The original design of the post office proposed a small airport on the building's roof, thus ensuring the swiftness of airmail service.

W2
GATEWAY CENTER IV
300 South Riverside Plaza
Skidmore, Owings & Merrill, 1983

A green mirrored glass curtain wall sheathes the 22-story steel structure of this office building by Skidmore design partner James DeStefano. The most outstanding aspect of the design is the eye-catching curvilinear facade, which complements the bend in the river. The best views of the building are from the Jackson and Van Buren bridges, but the entrance is surprisingly tucked into a small plaza on the building's west side. The lobby is of green Swiss marble.

W3
MID-AMERICA COMMODITY EXCHANGE
444 West Jackson
Skidmore, Owings & Merrill, 1972

Built over air rights of Union Station, this structure contains a trading room, 225 by 100 feet and 60 feet high, enclosed by green glass walls supported by an immense truss with exposed double diagonal bracing. The design is related to that of the John Hancock Building, built three years earlier.

W4
UNION STATION
210 South Canal
Graham, Anderson, Probst & White, 1913-25; Renovation, Lucien Lagrange Associates, 1992

Union Station, recently renovated, is the last of Chicago's grand old stations in the Roman revival style. Its heavy, stately colonnades provide pleasing rhythms, while the interior sky-lighted waiting space, covered in travertine, recalls great Roman baths or basilicas.

W5
FLORSHEIM SHOE COMPANY
(Metropolitan Place)
130 South Canal
Shaw, Metz & Dolio, 1949

The Florsheim administration building's strongly horizontal design with white glazed brick and ribbon windows represents some of Chicago's best work of the 1940s. The building has recently been converted to condominium lofts.

W6
GATEWAY CENTER III
222 South Riverside Plaza
Skidmore, Owings & Merrill, 1972

The 35-story Gateway III contrasts with the buildings around it in that its exterior walls are concrete, although its interior frame is steel.

W7
GATEWAY CENTER I
10 South Riverside Plaza
Skidmore, Owings & Merrill, 1965

Bruce Graham and Robert Diamant designed the first two Gateway Center buildings as twin 22-story black steel and green glass curtain wall structures. The construction of Gateway Center I demonstrated one of the early steps by the respectable financial world toward a gradual western movement, which would finally gobble up the derelict cityscape of Skid Row, at the time, Chicago's hangout for drunks and homeless.

W8
GATEWAY CENTER II
120 South Riverside Plaza
Skidmore, Owings & Merrill, 1968

Gateway I and II are sister structures, balancing each other at the river's edge on either side of Monroe Street.

W9
525 WEST MADISON
Skidmore, Owings & Merrill, 1983

This Z-shaped office building, designed by Adrian Smith, is 24 stories sheathed in dark, blue-black opaque glass with green glass windows. Its base is of alternating bands of light and dark brown granite.

W10
ILLINOIS BELL TELEPHONE BUILDING
10 South Canal
Holabird & Root, 1971

At the time of its construction, this reinforced concrete grid structure was much admired.

W11
525 WEST MONROE
Skidmore, Owings & Merrill, 1983

The cone-shaped glazed skylight entry and the red detailing around the windows call attention to this polished office structure.

W12
HELLER INTERNATIONAL TOWER
500 West Monroe
Skidmore, Owings & Merrill, 1992

This granite-clad tower strongly contrasts with Skidmore's other work in the area. It is related visually, however, to other S.O.M. buildings, such as the NBC Tower and the AT&T Building. Like those structures, it borrows its strong verticals and stepped-back massing from the architecture of the 1920s.

HELLER INTERNATIONAL TOWER

CITICORP CENTER

W13
RIVERSIDE PLAZA

(Daily News Building)
2 North Riverside Plaza (400 West Madison)
Holabird & Root, 1929

Originally built for the *Chicago Daily News*, the 26-story lime-stone building was the first in Chicago to be built using air rights over railroad tracks. Parts of the building were can-tilevered over the tracks by using double 12-foot-deep gird-ers. The structure was also the first in Chicago to incorpo-rate a plaza for public use, located between the building and the river. Built in the late 1920s, just before the stock market crash, it is an excellent example of the Art Deco style, com-plete with vertical bands of windows, blocky setbacks, and geometric ornamental details. The central block is narrow and slab-like, while symmetrical wings frame it on either end, giving it a form which has sometimes reminded people of an armchair. The ceiling of the longitudinal grand lobby, painted by John Warner Norton, is a dynamic colorful com-position of interpenetrating geometric shapes interspersed with depictions of newspaper production.

W14
CITICORP CENTER

500 West Madison
Murphy/Jahn, 1987

The streamlined look of this cascading 40-story office tower surmounting the Northwestern Railway terminal was inspired by some of the streamlined shapes, although not the buildings, of the 1930s. Helmut Jahn had previously worked with inverted cascading shapes in his design for the annex to the Board of Trade. The dramatic waterfall effect is enhanced by the blue enameled aluminum sheathing alter-nating with blue and silver glass. One enters through a wide arch (of Sullivan proportions) into a light airy lobby with exposed tubular steel trussing. The monumental arch, the open truss-work, and the large amount of glazing relate the lobby design to traditional railway stations of the nineteenth century.

W15
MORTON INTERNATIONAL BUILDING

100 North Riverside Plaza
Perkins & Will, 1993

Called by Paul Gapp, "a thoroughly Chicago-style office tower," the Morton International Building displays its struc-tural character. The design by Ralph Johnson superbly dealt with such challenges as a long, narrow, irregular lot, a foun-dation which had to allow trains to continue their operation on the lower level, and a number of different clients' needs. The varying masses, strung along the river, to some extent reflect different functions: a five story parking unit, a 13-story south section with office space and computer floors for Ameritech, and a 36-story unit for Morton Thiokol with a clock-tower on the northern end. The design of the gray granite, glass and metal exterior incorporates complicated patterns of horizontals and verticals. The rooftop of the south end displays a cantilevered system of exposed steel trusses, which, while necessary to redistribute loads, also contribute to a dramatic image of the technological age.

W16
RIVER CENTER

(Butler Brothers Building #1)
111 North Canal
D. H. Burnham & Company, 1913

Praised by Lewis Mumford in 1927 as some of the best Chicago architecture, this 14-story brick building and its mate to the north make a bold structural statement, typifying the industrial character of Chicago's near west side, The broad piers of each structure carry one's eye upward to cli-max in a Romanesque-style parapet. Both structures have stately Greek Doric columns at their Randolph Street entrances, set "in antis", that is, recessed into the facade.

W17
RANDOLPH PLACE

(Butler Brothers Building #2)
165 North Canal
Graham, Anderson, Probst & White, 1922

The structure, now converted into luxury apartments, retains its appeal in spite of its off-white paint job, which loses the original warmth of material, so characteristic of early Chicago industrial architecture.

W18
PRESIDENTIAL TOWERS

555, 575, 605, 625 West Madison
Solomon Cordwell Buenz & Associates, 1986

Four 49-story towers, which loom over Chicago's West Loop area, are visually sterile and perhaps "totalitarian" in their regularity—the identical height, chamfered corners, and repetitious windows. The concept reminds one of LeCorbusier's schemes for immense cities, although the architectural style here is much less interesting. The monotony of the rusticated concrete structures is broken only by their diagonal arrangement across the two-block site, which used to be Chicago's "Skid Row". The project has also been criticized because it was built with federal funds, although none of the 2,346 rental units are accessible to the poor. Residents are primarily single young "Yuppies" in their 30s who work in the Loop, who can walk to work if they choose.

W19
HAROLD WASHINGTON SOCIAL SECURITY ADMINISTRATION BUILDING

600 West Madison
Lester B. Knight & Associates, 1976

This ten-story office building has precast concrete utility cores which contrast with its mirrored glass curtain walls. In front of the building stands Claes Oldenburg's 101-foot-tall metal *Bat Column.*

W20
IIT-KENT COLLEGE OF LAW

565 West Adams
Holabird & Root, 1992

Particularly interesting in the design of this structure is the lamella truss ceiling of the reading on the top floor.

W21
ST. PATRICK'S CHURCH

140 South Desplaines
Carter & Bauer, 1852, 1856

Chicago's oldest church is a curious mixture of Norman Romanesque details such as the decorative blind arches and the single spire, which contrasts with the eastern-style onion dome.

PRESIDENTIAL TOWERS

N

W24
EISENHOWER EXPRESSWAY
CONGRESS

HARRISON

W22

W25a W25e

W25f

W25b

POLK
W25c

MORGAN

W26

HALSTED

W23

DAN RYAN EXPRESSWAY

W25d TAYLOR

DESPLAINES

JEFFERSON

CLINTON

CANAL

W25g

W27

W28 ROOSEVELT

W29

W22
GREYHOUND TERMINAL
630 West Harrison

W23
NORTHERN TRUST
COMPANY OPERATIONS
CENTER
801 South Canal

W24
RELIABLE BUILDING
1001 West Van Buren

W25
UNIVERSITY OF ILLINOIS AT
CHICAGO
*Harrison, Halsted, Roosevelt
and Morgan Streets*

W25a
UNIVERSITY HALL
601 South Morgan

W25b
UNIVERSITY LIBRARY
801 South Morgan

W25c
CHICAGO CIRCLE CENTER
710 South Halsted

W25d
SCIENCE AND
ENGINEERING
LABORATORIES
840 West Taylor

W25e
ARCHITECTURE & ART
BUILDING
845 West Harrison

W25f
BEHAVIORAL SCIENCE
BUILDING
1007 West Harrison

W25g
SCIENCE & ENGINEERING
SOUTH
801 West Taylor

W26
HULL HOUSE
800 South Halsted

W27
ST. IGNATIUS COLLEGE
PREP
1076 West Roosevelt Road

W28
HOLY FAMILY CHURCH
1080 West Roosevelt Road

W29
ILLINOIS REGIONAL
LIBRARY FOR THE BLIND
AND PHYSICALLY
HANDICAPPED
1055 West Roosevelt Road

NEAR WEST SIDE

The Near West, primarily west of the Kennedy and Dan Ryan Expressways, including south of the Congress and west of the river, has also enjoyed considerable renovation since the 1960s, when the construction of University of Illinois began. Although the university's erection required ruthless demolition of the existing Italian neighborhood and spurred violent antagonism toward the university, the intervening years have proved ultimately successful for the district. The hospital complexes have greatly expanded; "Greek Town" on Halsted flourished partly because of the university; numerous townhouse complexes have been built; and many of the loft buildings in the vicinity of the Eisenhower Expressway have been transformed and converted into housing and office units.

GREYHOUND TERMINAL

NORTHERN TRUST COMPANY OPERATIONS CENTER

W22
GREYHOUND TERMINAL
630 West Harrison
Nagle, Hartray & Associates Ltd.

The terminal is a well-designed two-story structure enclosing 35,000 square feet of space under a cable suspension roof. The roof also covers two bus pull-in areas of 5,000 square feet each. The roof system was a logical means of spanning a large distance economically with only ten vertical supports. Since the terminal is near the intersection of the Dan Ryan and Congress Expressways, the building is viewed most often from the raised expressway, or roof level. Also on the roof level is a raised, sawtooth-shaped office structure, angled in the same direction as that of the bus stalls on the ground. At street level, one is confronted by a long banded brick wall which angles back to the entrance, paralleling the diagonals of the axis of the offices and the bus parking. The station's greatest disadvantage is its location, not easily accessed from the central Loop.

W23
NORTHERN TRUST COMPANY OPERATIONS CENTER
801 South Canal
Eckenhoff Saunders Architects, 1991

An ornamental grid of sandblasted patterns decorates the pre-cast concrete skin to enliven the long facades of this massive structure. The lobby, which contains a terraced glass block waterfall, is entered through a recessed entrance in the Canal Street facade. The office building serves as the workplace for 2700 employees.

W24
RELIABLE BUILDING
1001 West Van Buren
Anonymous Architect

The west, south and east walls, visible from the Eisenhower Expressway, were painted in 1984 by Richard Haas of New York to simulate undulating windowed walls.

W25
UNIVERSITY OF ILLINOIS AT CHICAGO

Harrison, Halsted, Roosevelt and Racine

The first Chicago campus of the University of Illinois was at Navy Pier. From the beginning, the location of the new campus was controversial, for the neighborhood near the original Hull House, of mixed ethnic background, but largely Italian in the 1960s, was demolished in spite of much local opposition, to allow space for the new construction. Most of the buildings were designed by Walter Netsch of Skidmore, Owings & Merrill. First, the 28-story administration building and some of the smaller classroom buildings were constructed with walls of concrete panels cast in decorative shapes with window areas of darkened glass. The buildings were connected by a dual-level walkway system, giving access on the ground and second floors. The walkways converged in an open amphitheater with large lecture halls below. The walkways were never a success, however, developing cracks caused by the icy conditions in winter and blocking the sun from much of the ground level of the campus. Today these are gone, leaving a brighter campus, but less logical in its general plan.

RELIABLE BUILDING

W25a
UNIVERSITY HALL

601 South Morgan
Skidmore, Owings & Merrill, 1965

The administration building is eye-catching because it is larger on top than at the bottom. Netsch claimed that the three vertical divisions, each marked by different window patterns, were based on the Golden Section; however, the proportions of the whole are disturbingly anti-classical.

W25b
UNIVERSITY LIBRARY

801 South Morgan
Skidmore, Owings & Merrill, 1965

This four-story rectangular structure of long proportions is entered from the ground or second story.

UNIVERSITY HALL

ARCHITECTURE & ART BUILDING

HULL HOUSE

W25c
CHICAGO CIRCLE CENTER
710 South Halsted
C.F. Murphy Associates, 1965

The Circle Center on the east side of the campus is opposite from and approximately the same size and shape as the library on the west. It has a circular bookstore in its center, and various types of cafeteria, exhibition, and other student facilities in its wings. This is the only building of the original core designed by a firm other than SOM.

W25d
SCIENCE AND ENGINEERING LABORATORIES
840 West Taylor
Skidmore, Owings & Merrill, 1965

One of the largest buildings of the original 1965 complex was this rectangular structure with widely-spaced, massive concrete pillars.

Walter Netsch introduced another visual theme to the campus in 1966 when he built three very distinctive buildings: Architecture and Art, Behavioral Science, and Science and Engineering. Because of their complexity, their multiple angles, and their contrast to the rest of the campus, these structures created much attention. The Architecture and Art Building was the cover on an issue of *Architectural Forum* in 1966. According to Netsch, these structures were based on his "field theory," a term he assigned to make his system seem more rational than in fact it was. The system involved floor plans and sometimes parts of the elevations based on a series of rotated squares, or eight-pointed star shapes, which could be repeated ad infinitum.

W25e
ARCHITECTURE & ART BUILDING
845 West Harrison
Skidmore, Owings & Merrill, 1966

The first field theory building was the Architecture and Art Building, of which only phase one was built. The structure is beautiful as an angular geometric sculpture, but far from successful functionally. In the first few months of occupancy, students protested the building, claiming they needed more windows, and that they needed to be able to find their way to various locations. Walter Netsch met with them and explained that the building should be an adventure. Finally the controversy was forgotten, and the school learned to live with the inevitable problems.

W25f
BEHAVIORAL SCIENCE BUILDING
1007 West Harrison
Skidmore, Owings & Merrill, 1967

Perhaps this building is the most maze-like of any ever constructed. One might joke about its appropriateness for behavioral science.

W25g
SCIENCE & ENGINEERING SOUTH
801 West Taylor
Skidmore, Owings & Merrill, 1968

After the construction of this structure, the last and most extreme of the University of Illinois "field theory" buildings, Netsch modified his theory, becoming less rigid in the application of a predetermined geometry.

W26
HULL HOUSE

800 South Halsted
Anonymous Architect, 1856

Restored as a memorial to Jane Addams, who won the Nobel Peace Prize for her work here, Hull House is a beautiful brick Italianate structure with paired porch columns, paired slender arched windows, brackets, and a cupola. In 1889 when Jane Addams started the settlement house, the first of its kind in America, the neighborhood was a mixture of factories and crowded immigrant housing. Addams and her associates, mainly women, provided intellectual, social, cultural, spiritual and physical nourishment to the thousands of poor residents of the area. By 1907, twelve additional buildings had been constructed, all designed by Irving and Allen Pond. Except for the dining hall, which was moved and now functions as office and display space, the Pond and Pond buildings were demolished when the University of Illinois was built.

W27
ST. IGNATIUS COLLEGE PREP

(St. Ignatius College)
1076 West Roosevelt Rd.
Toussaint Menard, 1866-74; Addition: James J. Egan, 1895

This attractive Italianate structure of red brick walls and limestone base and trim is somewhat eclectic with its French-style split staircase, its decorative quoins, its steep gable and hipped roof. There is a strong vertical emphasis, especially in the double-story, arched windows at the top.

W28
HOLY FAMILY CHURCH

1080 West Roosevelt Road
Attr. to Dillenburg & Zucher, 1857-59; John M. Van Osdel, facade & interior, 1860

Chicago's second oldest church, which survived the fire of 1871, is a Gothic structure with a particularly fine interior. When threatened with the possibility of demolition, its parishioners and preservationists fought to save the church and finally won. Restoration was undertaken in 1991.

W29
ILLINOIS REGIONAL LIBRARY FOR THE BLIND AND PHYSICALLY HANDICAPPED

1055 West Roosevelt Road
Stanley Tigerman & Associates, 1975-78

The most distinctive exterior elevation is an extensive poured concrete wall pierced by a long undulating window. The lowest part of the window is the appropriate height for someone in a wheelchair. Other exterior walls are faced with red enameled steel panels. The inside, which houses a state center for Braille materials and a city library for the blind and physically handicapped, is designed with flowing curvilinear spaces, soft corners, and easy wheelchair access. Vivid primary colors are used throughout: red wall panels, yellow structural elements, and blue ducts and conduits. One wonders how well a handicapped person can operate in a structure with so many structural surprises! What a pity that the blind visitor would miss so much!

ST. IGNATIUS COLLEGE

ILLINOIS REGIONAL LIBRARY FOR THE BLIND AND PHYSICALLY HANDICAPPED

RECOMMENDED READINGS AND VIDEOS

Blaser, After Mies. *After Mies*. New York: Van Nostrand Reinhold, 1977.

Bluestone, Daniel. *Constructing Chicago*. New Haven: Yale University Press, 1991.

Bruegmann, Robert. *Holabird & Roche and Holabird & Root*. New York: Garland, 1991.

Chappell, Sally. *Architecture and Planning of Graham, Anderson, Probst and White, 1912-1920*. Chicago: University of Chicago Press, 1992.

Condit, Carl. *The Chicago School of Architecture*. Chicago: University of Chicago Press, 1964.

Glibota, Ante and Edelmann, Frederic (eds.) *Chicago. 150 Years of Architecture*. Paris: Paris Art Center, 1984.

Hines, Thomas. *Burnham of Chicago*. New York: Oxford University Press, 1974.

Jordiche, Joachim. *Helmut Jahn: Design of a New Architecture*. New York: Nichols Publishing Company, 1987.

Mayer, Harold M. and Richard C. Wade. *Chicago. Growth of a Metropolis*. Chicago: University of Chicago Press, 1969.

Saliga, Pauline, ed. *The Sky's the Limit: A Century of Chicago Skyscrapers*. New York: Rizzoli, 1990.

Schulze, Franz. *Mies Van der Rohe. A Critical Biography*. Chicago: University of Chicago Press, 1985.

Sinkevitch, Alice (ed.). *AIA Guide to Chicago*. San Diego: Harcourt Brace & Company, 1993.

Skyline Chicago video series, with guidebooks by Judith Paine McBrien, Perspectives International, 1991.

Stamper, John W. *Chicago's North Michigan Avenue: Planning and Development, 1900-1930*. Chicago: University of Chicago Press, 1991.

Twombly, Robert. *Louis Sullivan. His Life and Work*. Chicago: University of Chicago Press, 1986.

Zukowsky, John (ed.). *Chicago Architecture. 1872-1922. Birth of a Metropolis*. Munich: Prestel-Verlag, 1987.

_____. *Architecture and Design. 1923-1993. Reconfiguration of an American Metropolis*. Munich: Prestel-Verlag, 1993.

TOURS

Excellent tours are given by the Chicago Architectural Foundation, 224 South Michigan, Chicago, IL 60604. (312) 922-1742. Especially recommended is the boat tour on the Chicago River.